17·1·98

*Alan JudGiet*

# TEST YOUR OWN
# APTITUDE

# TEST
# YOUR OWN
# APTITUDE

## Second edition

## JIM BARRETT AND
## GEOFF WILLIAMS

KOGAN
PAGE

First published in Great Britain in hardback in 1980 by
Kogan Page Limited, 120 Pentonville Road,
London N1 9JN. Paperback edition 1980, Futura Publications.

Second edition 1990, published by Kogan Page Limited.

**British Library Cataloguing in Publication Data**
A CIP record for this book is available
from the British Library.

1876

ISBN 1-85091-918-6
ISBN 1-85091-919-4 Pbk

Typeset by DP Photosetting, Aylesbury, Bucks
Printed and bound in Great Britain by
Biddles Ltd, Guildford

# Contents

# Chapter 1
# Taking Stock 1: Who am I?

This book is designed as a self-help guide for everyone who wants a successful career. It is founded on solid scientific research and good psychological practice, but it is also a book which is intended to give you some fun. Combining a serious objective with having fun is part of our whole approach. In the same way, there is no reason why your career should not be fun; in fact, there is plenty of evidence to suggest that if you do have fun at work you are probably more productive as well. So if you are down in the dumps about your career – either because you do not know what to do or because you are bored – read on. We believe that what you do is largely up to you. If you are not happy with your present situation, change it. This book intends to help you to do whatever you want with your career.

This book is aimed principally at two groups of people: those who have not yet started on a career and those who have had at least one job but still do not feel that they are in the career which really suits them. But it could be that you belong to a third group who just enjoy a book like this – perhaps you combine pleasure with just 'checking up on yourself'.

Whatever your reasons for reading the book, it can help you to make better decisions about what you should do in the future. It is a sad fact that most people stumble into jobs – sad because unless people find a job which suits them they will never have the opportunity to use their potential. It is also a waste of human resources and a likely cause of frustration and stress at a personal level. There is all too often an unplanned move from school to college and then on to a professional qualification. Sometimes people go straight from school to jobs in the vicinity, no matter how unique their individual potential nor how restricted the range of local opportunities. People often go for the job which seems to offer them the most money or the greatest security in the short term, and are completely unaware of how their own psychology might be at odds with the job in the longer term. Other people 'follow in father's footsteps'; or maybe they abide by what parents, school or friends expect.

When you come to choose a career you should be aware of two things: first, you should know yourself and second, you should know what the world offers. In the end, your own success and happiness – however you measure these things – are determined by you. What makes somebody else content in a career will not necessarily apply to you. This is the time for you to make decisions on your own personal choices by establishing what you can do best and what you want to do most.

This book will help you to structure your career planning. 'Structure' is the key word and, if you follow the approach outlined here, you will make better informed and ultimately more creative career choices. You should work through and apply the three structured models of career/potential matching and give yourself a framework which will allow you to clarify (or sensibly scotch, your plans for developing yourself in your career. When you have worked through the various exercises which form the bulk of the book you can eventually put it all together in Chapter 5, Taking Stock 2.

The tests and questionnaires will give you an idea of what you can naturally do best (abilities), what suits your style and behaviour (personality), and what is likely to stimulate your interests and attitudes (motivation). The relevance of this basic information to your occupational decisions is then explained. More than quickly pinpointing the ideal career for you, this information is intended to provide a structured system for your own critical self-assessment. This will be of continuing service to you because the natural potential the tests elicit does not change much over time. The results will also be relevant even though changing technology may alter some career prospects.

## Structure of abilities

What we are seeking to establish is the real you. This is the person you want to be and not necessarily the person you are now. It is what you could become if you 'self-actualised'. This is why we often use the word 'ability' which has a special meaning in psychology, referring to your natural potential as well as what you can do after training. Ability is a reservoir of potential. Maybe your experience to date has not given your true ability a chance to come through.

The ability tests seek to identify those talents which are not solely dependent on learning and knowledge. In testing your underlying ability you may well discover some aptitude which you have not yet exploited and which could be developed.

It is not always easy for a lay person to understand how ability tests reveal anything about performance in the real world. What the tests do is to sample certain ways of comprehension, reasoning and problem-solving. The tests themselves will seem removed from the ordinary daily routine but, in fact, they sample the same potential which is needed in the real world. It is probably self-evident that all human endeavour, whether it be building bridges, voyaging in space or creating poetry, is an expression of electrical and chemical connections which take place in a person's mind!

As the ability tests minimise the emphasis which is so often placed upon education and qualifications, deductions can be made, such as 'This person has a level of reasoning ability which is higher than the average for science undergraduates.' Given information of this kind, it is fair to predict that the person in question could take a science degree, provided that other factors such as educational opportunity were present. Also important when taking a science degree is of course the element of motivation. However, if our potential seems greater for arts subjects than for science it seems practical to stop wasting time doing something which is going to give us a mediocre result when developing our stronger potential could bring us greater success.

Tests are extremely useful in revealing what a person can do. They are not so good at showing what a person cannot do

– simply because determination really can move mountains. It is enough to say that over the years tests have proved excellent predictors of an individual's performance and the type of work at which he or she is likely to excel. This is a significant advance on the old IQ test which simply gave a figure that did not mean a great deal by itself. Thus, the fact that you and I both have IQ scores of 100 (average) does not really help us very much because your 100 will be completely different from mine. You may get a 100 because you are good at arithmetic while I may get a 100 because I am good at seeing how mechanical things work. It is our differences which describe us, not our similarities, and it is our differences we must observe if we are going to locate these properly in the jigsaw puzzle which is the world of work.

The structured model we use provides you with basic information on all the major areas of underlying potential. Your relative strength in these tests can reveal an enormous amount relating to the type of education, training and work in which you are going to perform most quickly and successfully. It follows as well that you are likely to be happiest doing what you have the potential to do best. Perhaps the major cause of discontent at work is when people feel they have abilities which cannot be used in what they are doing.

## Structure of personality

In most occupations abilities can only be used effectively if certain dispositional and behavioural characteristics also exist. The mathematician needs discipline as well as intelligence; a social worker needs to be a logical thinker but selflessness, consideration and patience are more important; the business manager may need to be numerate but also needs to be assertive as well as empathetic. The personality and motivation chapters (Chapters 3 and 4) must therefore be treated as seriously as the abilities chapter (Chapter 2).

Human beings are extremely flexible in terms of the conditions as well as the relationships they are prepared to tolerate. Sometimes they will deceive themselves as much as they deceive others by pretending that they are putting up with something because they really want to. People often toil for years in situations which do not suit their personality. In circumstances of slavery or serfdom, personality was irrelevant. But this is not the case in today's world and organisations of all kinds, both in the public and private sectors, are increasingly taking the personality of employees into account.

It is now well known that the productive output of an organisation is influenced by the extent to which a personality is suited to the work in hand. When this is not the case, there tends to be internal friction between employees, with a consequent loss of output. It does not matter whether by 'productive' we mean the quantity of what is actually produced or the work atmosphere: bad quality atmosphere leads to bad quality products, whereas output and quality go up when people are happy.

Personality is therefore important, even though this may not be apparent in the short term since most of us can tolerate stresses and strains for a while. It is in the long term and for our own well being that we need work which is suited to our personality.

It is sometimes thought that personality changes and that we could therefore all adapt ourselves to any kind of work. But the idea that the situation creates the person is largely erroneous because over time people will tend to gravitate to work which suits them. The fact that our personality remains constant is shown in the fact that we know each other and know what to expect of each other. Our personality is as enduring as our physical characteristics. Although the most dramatic changes of personality take place as we mature into adulthood, there are still parts of ourselves that remain constant, even from childhood. We do change, but the changes brought about as the result of experience usually take place very slowly. All who read this book will have constant personality elements with which they and others are familiar and which will continue to define their potential for some time.

Tests of personality usually take the form of questions about private thoughts, feelings and ways of behaving. This is where you have to be honest if you want a realistic appraisal of your capabilities. Personality tests are different from ability tests because there are no right or wrong answers. What emerges is simply right for you because it is the real you. Although you might wish you were endowed with characteristics you do not have, perhaps because you admire those characteristics in others, it may be helpful to remind yourself that those people may see something which they admire in you. For example, people frequently say that they wish they were more extroverted, because they want to be more sociable at parties, able to stand up and make a speech, popular and the centre of attention. Ironically, we have found that the extrovert often admires people with a reflective and perhaps more studious temperament, feeling that introverts achieve more in meaningful ways.

As with the structure of the ability model, the personality model provides a descriptive framework of personality which gives you practical 'plugs' for relating your temperament to different careers in a systematic and objective process.

## Structure of motivation

If you ask people what they are really interested in doing they may feel that they know the answer. These are among the lucky few! Most people are unsure and usually it is either because they do not know their own potential or because they do not know what opportunities exist for them. Some people have 'pie in the sky' ideas, in which they feel they might be miraculously transported to a situation where they are famous or rich or leading a more exciting life.

The motivational tests are helpful in showing you where you may be getting your ambitions completely wrong. The structured model we use looks beneath your temporary interests and beyond your (perhaps) limited knowledge of careers because it allows you to express some measure of your underlying aspirations against the whole range of possibilities.

Whether you are still young and have yet to start out on a career or whether you are now rethinking your career, your underlying interests will have some firmness and remain constant over time. It is true that, as with personality, a person's interests change as they mature. In the early part of your life your interests may have been dictated by access to particular experiences or kinds of information or by encouragement from parents or close friends. Without some form of proper comparison – which is what the motivational model provides – many of us think that, given the opportunity, we could perform just as well as a famous singer, make better decisions than certain politicians, write books, grow flowers, make discoveries, help others or perhaps get away from it all – the possibilities are endless. The key thing is to establish what you are really interested in, then you are likely to do it well and experience satisfaction. People are sometimes uncertain how strong their interests really are; our structured objective system will help you to consider lots of possibilities and then show you how strongly you feel about one type of career or another.

You will find that the tests of motivation are often deceptively simple, such as asking you to choose the job which you prefer out of a pair. You will also be asked what sort of activities appeal to you and perhaps this will stop you from saying at the outset, 'Oh, I couldn't do that' or 'I'd never get the qualifications for that', which may not, in the end, be fair comments to make about yourself. If we establish what appeals to you first of all without imposing limitations, the other structured results of personality and ability can help to determine how far and in what manner you should travel down one career route as opposed to another.

## Are there some things which tests cannot measure?

There may be numerous factors which could be important for special forms of work or even in particular situations at work but the structured approach given in this book will be sufficient in providing an overall guide. Otherwise there are general considerations which need to be taken into account before you make any firm decisions about what you are going to do.

First, you will have to bear in mind that some careers demand physical characteristics which you do not have.

Second, you might find a career which is ideal for you, but have to face the fact that it is impossible to obtain the qualification required because the educational system will not permit entry at your age. The circumstances in which you find yourself are likely to be the most important factor. By circumstances we mean where you live, your family ties, and so on, all of which must be borne in mind. For example, there may be many factors to prevent a person from dropping everything and setting off to pursue a lifelong ambition. It is not to say that circumstances are always negative or will always tie you down – it is sometimes a matter of sorting out what is going to be most important to you at any given time. However, it stands to reason that it may not be possible to achieve one thing at the expense of another.

Those people who are rethinking their career will experience more difficulty than those just starting out because their circumstances are likely to be more complicated. People in mid-career frequently encounter a risk factor associated with giving up a job and the consequent stresses on a dependent family as well as other social and economic difficulties. Many people feel that relative discontent with some aspects of work is a small price to pay for family security and happiness. It is sometimes a question of making a compromise but compromising with full awareness is often better than simply 'putting up with' a situation because you feel there is no choice. In fact, there is always a choice and the assessment of yourself should ultimately consist of sorting out the relative importance of your present circumstances in line with the information derived from the structured analysis of yourself.

We believe that the information you will gain about yourself from working through this book will be beneficial. It is better to have information than not to have it; and you are not obliged to do anything with it.

When faced with test and quesionnaire results, it is sensible to ask whether the results seem logical and 'fit' you well, however surprising they may be. This does not imply that the tests will tell you what you know already. Instead, they will tend to show up more explicit ideas, assumptions, feelings and capabilities which you may long have been aware of, but which you have been keeping at the back of your mind or perhaps even hiding from yourself.

To sum up, the approach used in this book can give you valuable insight into ways in which your potential may be used more effectively. It can be an extremely useful objective check for those in mid-career; it can be useful for young people requiring guidance on the kind of education which would suit them best and on the type of career in which they would be most successful; it can also be valuable for people considering second careers. As we have already said, although it is a serious book, you can have fun with it and our intention is that, whoever you are and whatever you want, the outcome will be positive for you.

# Chapter 2
# Abilities: What Can I Do?

Our abilities are a mixture of our underlying natural ability and our experience and attainment.

You already know a great deal about your attainment, that is, the kind of qualifications you already possess and the experience that you gained in acquiring them. From this you know what kind of activities you find easiest and which you find most difficult.

Unfortunately, however, many people do not always choose the right subjects at school, the right subjects being those which we can study most easily. All too frequently our choices are determined by other considerations such as how much we like and respect various teachers, how good they are as teachers, what subjects our parents and friends think are most 'suitable' and, of course, what options are offered by the school. Once we have started to specialise it becomes increasingly difficult to have a clear idea of what else might be available.

In this book we are more concerned with our underlying abilities, that is, the way we naturally approach problems and difficulties and our innate methods of reasoning. Some of these abilities relate quite well to academic subjects while others do not. Thus, although we may find that our abilities match the subjects we have enjoyed and completed, we may also find some 'hidden' talents which we have not yet fully explored.

Most of us can do most subjects to a greater or lesser extent. The major differences are shown by the ease with which we can cope with new problems in a particular area. Also, we can often disguise weakness in an ability if we have considerable determination and perseverance.

We are likely to be more productive, however, if we are using our best abilities to their fullest extent rather than relying on those which are not so strong. These are best left as supporters. In this way we use the minimum energy to gain the maximum benefit. In career terms this means that we are likely to move faster and further than if we are constantly having to struggle to keep up.

## The ability tests

The ability tests are a series of tests to be completed in a particular time limit. This will give you an idea of how powerful you are when having to reason in this area. If you had unlimited time you could probably complete most of the questions accurately but this would give very little idea of which way of reasoning was the most suitable and easiest for you. Therefore, be strict with yourself about the time limits.

All the tests are based on ten-minute slots although in the acuity test there are two parts, each five minutes long.

We strongly recommend that you complete all the tests before finding out how you have done and, wherever possible, try to complete the tests all in one go. This means that you will need between an hour and a half and two hours to read the instructions, do the practice examples and complete the tests.

Before each of the tests there are some practice questions to give you an idea of what to expect. Obviously, the questions in the main tests become somewhat more difficult! But please make sure that you understand the examples before starting the test proper.

As with all the test questionnaires in this book you are able to make the results different from what is accurate. Please remember, you are only cheating yourself if you do not take them seriously.

# Verbal reasoning

This test is to see how you reason with words.

*For each question there are four alternative answers. Circle the one which you think is correct. There are different types of question and here are a few to try.*

*The first one has been done for you to show you how to mark the answer.*

## Sample questions

1. Boy is to Man as Girl is to
   (a) Elephant   (b) Children   (c) Woman   (d) Horse

2. Rock means
   (a) Stone   (b) Mountain   (c) Roll   (d) Water

3. Tractor is to Trailer as Horse is to
   (a) Stable   (b) Cart   (c) Saddle   (d) Engine

4. North is the opposite of
   (a) South   (b) East   (c) Cold   (d) Hot

5. What is a Stable?
   (a) Pasture   (b) Horse   (c) Fountain   (d) Building

*Now turn over for the answers.*

---

Now you can start the full test which begins on the next page, You have *10 minutes* to do as much as you can. You must work as accurately as you can and as fast as you can. When you are ready, start the clock and begin.

---

# Testing verbal reasoning

1. Ocean is to Pond as Deep is to
   (a) Shallow   (b) Well   (c) Sea   (d) Lake

2. Early is the opposite of
   (a) Evening   (b) Late   (c) Postpone   (d) Breakfast

3. Man is to Masculine As Woman is to
   (a) Intuitive   (b) Madam   (c) Girl   (d) Feminine

4. What does Frozen mean?
   (a) Glued   (b) Liquid   (c) Solid   (d) Water

5. Circle is to Sphere as Square is to
   (a) Ball   (b) Cube   (c) Polygon   (d) Triangle

6. Army is to land as Navy is to
   (a) Sea   (b) Mountains   (c) Ships   (d) RAF

7. What means the same as Portion?
   (a) Whole   (b) Part   (c) Chip   (d) None

8. Sock is to Foot as Hat is to
   (a) Band   (b) Hair   (c) Head   (d) Face

9. What does Solitary mean?
   (a) Crowd   (b) Diamond   (c) Partner   (d) Alone

10. Wise is to Foolish as Vain is to
    (a) Modest   (b) Pretty   (c) Conceit   (d) Proud

11. Dynamic is the opposite of
    (a) Electrical   (b) Tardy   (c) Static   (d) Resistant

12. Horse is to Jockey as Car is to
    (a) Vehicle   (b) Butler   (c) Cart   (d) Chauffeur

13. Acquiesce is the opposite of
    (a) Clumsy   (b) Obstacle   (c) Quit   (d) Protest

14. What does Debate mean?
    (a) Comment   (b) Talk   (c) Argue   (d) Create

15. Which would be third in alphabetical order?
    (a) Sevene   (b) Severn   (c) Seveen   (d) Seven

# Answers to sample questions on page 18

1. (c)
2. (a)
3. (b)
4. (a)
5. (d)

*Check your answers. If you have made a mistake look at the question again to see, if you can, where you went wrong.*

16. Sentence is to Paragraph as Word is to
    (a) Letter  (b) Sentence  (c) Paragraph  (d) Phrase

17. Which is the odd one out?
    (a) Speech  (b) Peroration  (c) Aside  (d) Saunter

18. Eagle is to Sparrow as Alsation is to
    (a) Corgi  (b) Retriever  (c) Fox  (d) St Bernard

19. Which is the odd one out?
    (a) Seminal  (b) Germane  (c) Propagative  (d) Derivative

20. Which is the penultimate letter to the word REST?
    (a) R  (b) E  (c) S  (d) T

21. What is a Turbine?
    (a) Fish  (b) Engine  (c) Tower  (d) String

22. Capital is to Interest as Labour is to
    (a) Conservative  (b) Wages  (c) Authority
    (d) Machinery.

23. Never is to Seldom as Always is to
    (a) Occasional  (b) Usual  (c) Often  (d) Every time

24. Certainty is the opposite of
    (a) Correctness  (b) Precision  (c) Dubiety  (d) Infinite

25. Which is the odd one out?
    (a) Terse  (b) Compact  (c) Angry  (d) Curt

26. Bolt is to Nut as Hook is to
    (a) Screw  (b) Eye  (c) Door  (d) Grass

27. Which is the odd one out?
    (a) Lock  (b) Quay  (c) Bollard  (d) Anchor

28. Heredity is to Environment as Nature is to
    (a) Nurture  (b) Ancestry  (c) Health  (d) Animal

29. What is an Edifice?
    (a) Building  (b) Illness  (c) Boatyard  (d) Executive

30. Scabbard is to Sword as Arrow is to
    (a) Tourniquet  (b) Sheath  (c) String  (d) Quiver

31. Feather is to Bird as Fence is to
    (a) Farm  (b) Stake  (c) Hedge  (d) Warehouse

32. Irascible is the opposite of
    (a) Striking  (b) Flamboyant  (c) Irritable  (d) Phlegmatic

33. Nurse is to Doctor as Secretary is to
    (a) Dentist  (b) Typewriter  (c) Executive  (d) Desk

34. Which is the odd one out?
    (a) Marriage  (b) Annul  (d) Divorce  (d) Separation

35. Which is the odd one out?
    (a) Dog  (b) Hunt  (c) Fox  (d) Stalk

36. Colour is to Bleach as Flushed is to
    (a) Blush  (b) Roseate  (c) Watered  (d) Wan

37. Stint is the opposite of
    (a) Surfeit  (b) Prolix  (c) Meticulous  (d) Splint

38. Which is the odd one out?
    (a) Foam  (b) Mush  (c) Bubbles  (d) Surf

39. Which is the odd one out?
    (a) Pretence  (b) Subterfuge  (c) Moonshine
    (d) Reluctance

40. Direct is to Tortuous as Dilatory is to
    (a) Expeditious  (b) Straight  (c) Curved
    (d) Circumlocutory

41. Where is to Lounge as When is to
    (a) Stand  (b) Time  (c) Soon  (d) How

42. Which is the odd one out?
    (a) Stand  (b) Vegetate  (c) Prevail  (d) Subsist

Finish

*PLEASE COMPLETE ALL THE TESTS BEFORE LOOKING AT THE ANSWERS.*

# Numerical reasoning

This test assesses how easily you think with numbers.

*The test consists of numbers which go together in some way to form a series. You have to see how they go together and then choose the next number from the four answers. When you find the correct answer circle it or put a cross through it.*

Try these. The first one has been done for you.

## Sample questions

1. 1  2  3  4  5          (a)6  (b)7  (c)5  (d)10

2. 12  10  8  6  4          (a)3  (b)2  (c)1  (d)0

3. 2  4  8  16  32          (a)56  (b)72  (c)144  (d)64

4. 3  4  6  9  13          (a)15  (b)18  (c)17  (d)20

5. 1  1  2  3  5          (a)7  (b)10  (c)8  (d)9

6. 729  243  81  27  9          (a)3  (b)4½  (c)6  (d)–18

*Now turn over for the answers.*

## Answers

1. (a)
2. (b)
3. (d)
4. (b)
5. (c)
6. (a)

*Check your answers. If you have made a mistake look at the question again to see, if you can, where you went wrong.*

Now you can start the full test which begins on the next page. You have *10 minutes* to do as much as you can. You must work as accurately as you can and as fast as you can. When you are ready, start the clock and begin.

# Testing numerical reasoning

1. 1 3 5 7 9          (a)8 (b)11 (c)12 (d)13

2. ½ 1 2 4 8        (a)12 (b)24 (c)16 (d)18

3. 3 5 8 12 17      (a)25 (b)26 (c)22 (d)23

4. 2 2 4 6 10       (a)14 (b)10 (c)20 (d)16

5. 4 8 16 32 64     (a)96 (b)100 (c)128 (d)112

6. 81 27 9 3 1      (a)½ (b)1 (c)⅓ (d)⅙

7. 0.1 0.3 0.5 0.7 0.9  (a)1.1 (b)0.11 (c)11 (d)0.011

8. 1 4 9 16 25      (a)32 (b)36 (c)48 (d)49

9. 5 9 17 33 65     (a)101 (b)108 (c)143 (d)129

10. 0 3 8 15 24      (a)36 (b)30 (c)35 (d)31

11. 1 8 27 64 125    (a)250 (b)216 (c)185 (d)196

12. 5 7 11 17 25     (a)35 (b)27 (c)31 (d)39

13. 4 5 7 11 19      (a)33 (b)27 (c)37 (d)35

14. 0 3 2 5 4        (a)8 (b)7 (c)9 (d)6

15. 0 8 8 16 24      (a)40 (b)24 (c)32 (d)48

16. 2 5 11 23 47     (a)80 (b)95 (c)92 (d)101

17. 10 25 12 30 14   (a)16 (b)50 (c)24 (d)35

18. 3 9 6 15 9       (a)8 (b)15 (c)12 (d)21

19. 50 40 100 90 150  (a)200 (b)180 (c)140 (d)300

20. 2 4 4 16 16      (a)32 (b)64 (c)24 (d)196

21. 15 9 24 33 57     (a)80 (b)90 (c)89 (d)48

Finish

*PLEASE COMPLETE ALL THE TESTS BEFORE LOOKING AT THE ANSWERS.*

## Perceptual reasoning

This test looks at how easily you can reason with symbols and shapes.

*After each question there are four answers and, when you have found the correct answer, put a circle around, or cross out, your choice. The first one has been completed for you.*

## Sample questions

*Now turn over for the answers.*

Now you can start the full test which begins on the next page. You have *10 minutes* to do as much as you can. You must work as accurately as you can and as fast as you can. When you are ready, start the clock and begin.

# Testing perceptual reasoning

1. ○ ● □    ■ ○ ⊠ ▲
      is to    as    is to    (a)    (b)    (c)    (d)

2. which comes next?
      (a)    (b)    (c)    (d)

3. Which is the odd one out?
      (a)    (b)    (c)    (d)

4. [ + ] makes
      (a)    (b)    (c)    (d)

5. Which comes next?
      (a)    (b)    (c)    (d)

6. ⟺ is to ⟹ as ‖ is to ‖
      (a)    (b)    (c)    (d)

7. ○ + □ makes
      (a)    (b)    (c)    (d)

# Answers to sample questions on page 26

1. (b)
2. (c)
3. (c)
4. (a)
5. (a)

*Check your answers. If you have made a mistake look at the question again to see, if you can, where you went wrong.*

8. Which comes next?    (a) (b) (c) (d)

9. Which is the odd one out?    (a) (b) (c) (d)

10. ⌐ is to ⌐ as ↗ is to    (a) (b) (c) (d)

11. ⋈ + ⋈ makes    (a) (b) (c) (d)

12. Which is the odd one out?    (a) (b) (c) (d)

13. Which comes next?    (a) (b) (c) (d)

14. ⊡ is to ⊙ as ⊡ is to    (a) (b) (c) (d)

15.

Which is the odd one out?

(a) (b) (c) (d)

16.

Which comes next?

(a) (b) (c) (d)

17.

is to    as    is to

(a) (b) (c) (d)

18.

Which comes next?

(a) (b) (c) (d)

19. + makes

(a) (b) (c) (d)

20. Which is the odd one out?

(a) (b) (c) (d)

21.

Which comes next?

(a) (b) (c) (d)

22. + makes

(a) (b) (c) (d)

23.

Which is the odd one out? (a) (b) (c) (d)

24.

+ makes

(a) (b) (c) (d)

25.

is to ... as ... is to

(a) (b) (c) (d)

26.

Which comes next? (a) (b) (c) (d)

27.

+ makes

(a) (b) (c) (d)

28.

Which comes next? (a) (b) (c) (d)

29.

Which comes next? (a) (b) (c) (d)

30.

Which is the odd one out? (a) (b) (c) (d)

31. Which comes next?      (a)     (b)     (c)     (d)

32. ⊟ is to ⋃ as ⚭ is to    (a)     (b)     (c)     (d)

33. Which comes next?      (a)     (b)     (c)     (d)

34. Which is the odd one out?      (a)     (b)     (c)     (d)

35. Which comes next?      (a)     (b)     (c)     (d)

Finish

*PLEASE COMPLETE ALL THE TESTS BEFORE LOOKING AT THE ANSWERS.*

# Spatial ability

This test explores how easily you can 'see' and manipulate shapes and figures in space. Here you are not being asked to reason with the shapes but to move them through three dimensions as quickly as you can.

*You are to answer each question with a 'Y' for yes or possibly yes or 'N' for definitely no.*

*There are two types of question and here are some examples:*

## Type 1

Here you are given a plan of the three dimensional shape as if you were making it from a sheet of cardboard.

For instance, if you unfolded the cube

the shape you would get would be:

Following this plan are three or four models and you are to state whether or not each shape can be made from the plan.

## Type 2

This time you are given two shapes and the second is to be taken away from the first. Following these two shapes are three or four other shapes and you are to state whether or not this shape could be left.

## Sample questions

Put a circle around the correct answer for each question.

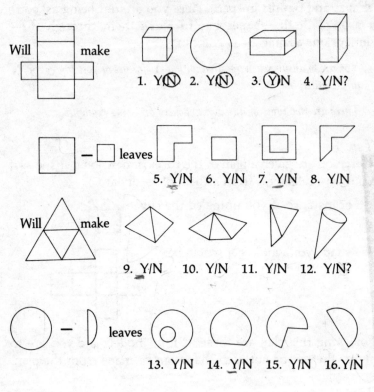

Will make

1. Y/N̶ 2. Y/N̶ 3. Ⓨ/N 4. Y/N?

— leaves

5. Y/N 6. Y/N 7. Y/N 8. Y/N

Will make

9. Y/N 10. Y/N 11. Y/N 12. Y/N?

— leaves

13. Y/N 14. Y/N 15. Y/N 16. Y/N

*Now turn over for the answers.*

Now you can start the full test which begins on the next page. You have *10 minutes* to do as much as you can. You must work as accurately as you can and as fast as you can. When you are ready, start the clock and begin.

# Testing spatial ability

A.

Will    make

1. Y/N   2. Y/N   3. Y/N   4. Y/N

B. Will

make   5. Y/N   6. Y/N   7. Y/N   8. Y/N

C.

— leaves

9. Y/N   10. Y/N   11. Y/N   12. Y/N

D. Will    make

13. Y/N   14. Y/N   15. Y/N   16. Y/N

E. Will    make

17. Y/N   18. Y/N   19. Y/N   20. Y/N

F.

— leaves

21. Y/N   22. Y/N   23. Y/N

# Answers to sample questions on page 34

| | |
|---|---|
| 1. N | 9. Y |
| 2. N | 10. N |
| 3. Y | 11. Y |
| 4. Y | 12. N |
| 5. Y | 13. N |
| 6. N | 14. Y |
| 7. Y | 15. N |
| 8. N | 16. N |

*Check your answers. If you have made a mistake look at the question again to see, if you can, where you went wrong.*

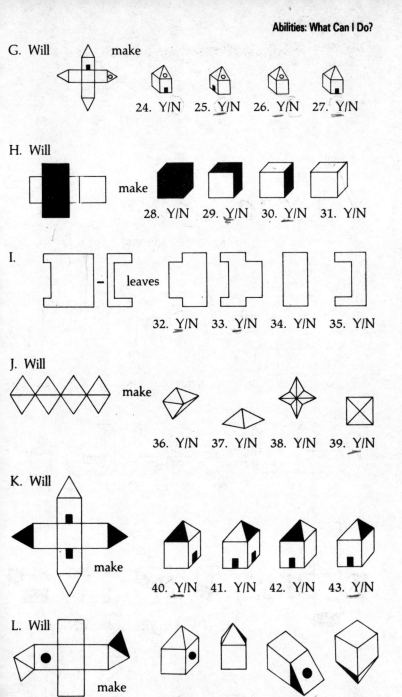

G. Will      make

24. Y/N    25. Y/N    26. Y/N    27. Y/N

H. Will      make

28. Y/N    29. Y/N    30. Y/N    31. Y/N

I.    – leaves

32. Y/N    33. Y/N    34. Y/N    35. Y/N

J. Will      make

36. Y/N    37. Y/N    38. Y/N    39. Y/N

K. Will      make

40. Y/N    41. Y/N    42. Y/N    43. Y/N

L. Will      make

44. Y/N    45. Y/N    46. Y/N    47. Y/N

37

M.

leaves

48. Y/N   49. Y/N   50. Y/N   51. Y/N

N. Will     make

52. Y/N   53. Y/N   54. Y/N   55. Y/N

O. Will     make

56. Y/N   57. Y/N   58. Y/N   59. Y/N

P.     leaves

60. Y/N   61. Y/N   62. Y/N   63. Y/N

Q.     folded makes

64. Y/N   65. Y/N   66. Y/N   67. Y/N

R.

folded makes

68. Y/N    69. Y/N    70. Y/N    71. Y/N

S.

leaves

72. Y/N    73. Y/N    74. Y/N    75. Y/N

Finish

*PLEASE COMPLETE ALL THE TESTS BEFORE LOOKING AT THE ANSWERS.*

# Technical ability

This test is to find out whether you have a 'feel' for mechanical and technical things. It explores whether or not you find it easy to understand how things work and function.

*Each written question has a diagram by it to give you the required information. Choose the correct answer from the choices given. Put a circle around, or cross out, the correct answer. The first one has been completed for you.*

## Sample questions

1.
Which arrow will balance the beam?
(a) A  (b) B  (c) C
(d) all equal

2.
Which chain will hold up the lantern?
(a) P  (b) Q  (c) R  (d) all equal

3.
If the driving wheel goes in the direction shown, which way will the second wheel turn?
(a) either  (b)  (c)

*Now turn over for the answers.*

Now you can start the full test which begins on the next page. You have *10 minutes* to do as much as you can. You must work as accurately as you can and as fast as you can. When you are ready, start the clock and begin.

# Testing technical ability

1.

If the wheel rotates as shown, P will
(a) move to the right and stop
(b) move to the left and stop
(c) move to and fro
(d) none of these

2.

Which arrow will balance the beam?
(a) A   (b) B   (c) C   (d) D

3.

When the two screws are turned the same amount as shown, the ball will move towards
(a) F   (b) G   (c) H   (d) J   (e) K

4.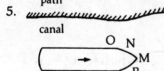

Which way does wheel X move?
(a) either   (b) ⌒   (c) ⌒
(d) stays still

5.

To move the boat easily in the direction shown, the rope would be best attached to
(a) M   (b) N   (c) O   (d) P
(e) Q

6.

Which nail is most likely to pull out of the wall?
(a) A   (b) B   (c) C
(d) all equally likely

## Answers to sample questions on page 40

1. (b)
2. (b)
3. (c)

*Check your answers. If you have made a mistake look at the question again to see, if you can, where you went wrong.*

---

7.

If each block weighs the same, which one will be most difficult to push over?
(a) A (b) B (c) C (d) D

8.

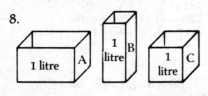

Which tank will cool water fastest?
(a) A (b) B (c) C
(d) all equal

9.

Which pendulum moves slowest?
(a) A (b) B (c) C
(d) all equal

10.

Which tent peg will give the best hold in soft ground?
(a) P (b) Q (c) R
(d) S (e) T

11.  Which weight will be easiest to lift?
(a) A  (b) B  (c) C
(d) all equal

12. If each rope in the above diagram is pulled at the same speed, which load will move slowest?
(a) A  (b) B  (c) C  (d) all equal

13. Which gear wheel goes in the same direction as the driver?
(a) X  (b) Y  (c) Z

14. Which gear goes round fastest?
(a) W  (b) X  (c) Y  (d) Z

15. Where is the cannonball most likely to land?
(a) A  (b) B  (c) C  (d) D

16. Which plank is most likely to break?
(a) A  (b) B  (c) either

17.  Which way will wheel Q turn?
(a) ⌢ (b) ⌢ (c) either

18.  If the handle is moved as shown, how will the hooks M and N move?
(a) M up, N down
(b) M down, N up
(c) M up, N up
(d) M down, N down
(e) M up, N still

19.  Which box is the heaviest?
(a) A   (b) B   (c) C   (d) all equal

20.  Which way will the black ball move when struck by the white ball in the direction shown?
(a) A   (b) B   (c) C   (d) D

21. The diameter of pulleys A and C is 10cm and pulleys B and D is 5cm. When pulley A makes a complete turn pulley D will turn
(a) once   (b) twice   (c) 4 times   (d) 6 times   (e) 8 times

22. If pulley D is the driver, which pulley turns slowest?
(a) A   (b) B   (c) C   (d) all the same

23.

If the drawing is of water pipes, which will carry the most water per metre length?
(a) A   (b) B   (c) C
(d) all equal

30cm     10cm    15cm

24. If the drawing is of electrical cable, which offers the most resistance per metre length?
(a) A   (b) B   (c) C   (d) all equal

25.

If the blocks are all of the same material, which is the heaviest?
(a) A   (b) B   (c) C
(d) all equal

26. Which has the greatest density?
(a) A   (b) B   (c) C   (d) all equal

27.

Which chain would support the weight by itself?
(a) any equally   (b) B   (c) C   (d) D

28. Which diagram shows the most likely path of a bomb falling from a moving aeroplane on a calm day?
(a) X   (b) Y   (c) Z

29.

Which way will the handle have to turn to raise the bucket?

(a) A   (b) B   (c) either

30.

Which of these would return to its present position when moved slightly?

(a) A   (b) B   (c) neither   (d) both

31.

Which boat has the safest anchorage?

32.

Which shape makes the best flywheel?

(a)       (b)       (c)

33.

Where is the pendulum moving fastest?

Finish

*PLEASE COMPLETE ALL THE TESTS BEFORE LOOKING AT THE ANSWERS.*

## Acuity skills

This test is to see how quickly and accurately you can complete clerical tasks. There are two parts to the test.

*Each part takes 5 minutes and you must time yourself accurately. The first part is simply sums using the four rules + − × ÷. For example:*

$$\begin{array}{r} 35 \\ 7+ \\ \hline 42 \end{array}$$

## Sample questions

| 1. | 26 | 2. | 35 | 3. | 74 |
|---|---|---|---|---|---|
| | 9+ | | 12− | | 7× |
| | — | | — | | — |

*In the second part you have three names and you are to find which one should come first if they were filed in alphabetical order. Put a cross through it. For example:*

(a) Jones  (b) J~~a~~s~~o~~n  (c) Joseph

## Sample questions

1. (a) Taylor  (b) Tailor  (c) Townsend

2. (a) Deader  (b) Dreader  (c) Dader

3. (a) Wisp  (b) Willow  (c) Wilter

*Now turn over for the answers.*

## Answer

*Part 1*
1. 35   2. 23   3. 518

*Part 2*
1. (b)   2. (c)   3. (b)

*Check your answers. If you have made a mistake look at the question again to see, if you can, where you went wrong.*

You must work as accurately as you can and as fast as you can. You have 5 *minutes* only on each part. When you have finished Part 1 go straight on to Part 2. As soon as you are ready start the clock and begin.

## Acuity test 1

Remember you only have 5 *minutes* for this part.

| 1. 24 5+ | 2. 71 9+ | 3. 35 69+ | 4. 45 62+ | 5. 15 19 23+ |
|---|---|---|---|---|
| 6. 26 6× | 7. 37 48 35+ | 8. 49 8× | 9. 64 57 62+ | 10. 48 13− |
| 11. 127 98− | 12. 35 9× | 13. 7)364 | 14. 28 364 479+ | 15. 3)369 |
| 16. 67 12+ | 17. 47 5× | 18. 249 158− | 19. 8)584 | 20. 6016 739− |

| 21. 279 | 22. 135 | 23. 37 | 24. | 25. 924 |
|---|---|---|---|---|
| 686 | 36– | 9× | 12)1452 | 536– |
| 755+ | | | | |

| 26. 612 | 27. 26 | 28. 23 | 29. 24 | 30. 916 |
|---|---|---|---|---|
| 387– | 15 | 83+ | 8× | 158– |
| | 83+ | | | |

| 31. 54 | 32. 67 | 33. 217 | 34. 43 | 35. |
|---|---|---|---|---|
| 36+ | 29+ | 138– | 11× | 6)3528 |

## Acuity test 2

*Put a cross through the name to be filed first. Remember, you have only 5 minutes for this part.*

| | | | |
|---|---|---|---|
| 1. | (a) Able | (b) Abel | (c) Abbel |
| 2. | (a) Tango | (b) Tanker | (c) Tabber |
| 3. | (a) Swift | (b) Switch | (c) Stuck |
| 4. | (a) Dean | (b) Deal | (c) Drift |
| 5. | (a) Frant | (b) French | (c) Freak |
| 6. | (a) Tranter | (b) Truck | (c) Tramper |
| 7. | (a) Grant | (b) Gant | (c) Great |
| 8. | (a) Willis | (b) Wiltshire | (c) Wilter |
| 9. | (a) Simons | (b) Simkins | (c) Simmons |
| 10. | (a) Stanley | (b) Sturdy | (c) Straemer |
| 11. | (a) Foster | (b) Forster | (c) Fortnum |
| 12. | (a) Yarrow | (b) Yaught | (c) Yammer |
| 13. | (a) Pear | (b) Pearce | (c) Pearson |
| 14. | (a) Burch | (b) Birch | (c) Brunch |
| 15. | (a) Fox | (b) Fotse | (c) Foray |

| | | |
|---|---|---|
| 16. (a) Hamilton | (b) Harding | (c) Hammer |
| 17. (a) Gough | (b) Guntler | (c) Goff |
| 18. (a) Pear | (b) Peirs | (c) Pedlar |
| 19. (a) Brown | (b) Browne | (c) Brownne |
| 20. (a) Milton | (b) Miller | (c) Milstone |
| 21. (a) Delafield | (b) Deldafield | (c) Delderfield |
| 22. (a) Johnson | (b) Johnstone | (c) Johnston |
| 23. (a) Jackron | (b) Jackson | (c) Jackman |
| 24. (a) Phillips | (b) Philips | (c) Phillippes |
| 25. (a) Crow | (b) Crout | (c) Crove |
| 26. (a) Mackie | (b) Mackensie | (c) Macky |
| 27. (a) Young | (b) Younger | (c) Youngest |
| 28. (a) Crispin | (b) Crist | (c) Crump |
| 29. (a) Wober | (b) Waller | (c) Walters |
| 30. (a) Katz | (b) Katin | (c) Kaarl |
| 31. (a) Davis | (b) Davies | (c) Davit |
| 32. (a) Mordecai | (b) Morden | (c) Mortimer |
| 33. (a) Butler | (b) Buwer | (c) Butcher |
| 34. (a) Stratford | (b) Stafford | (c) Strafford |
| 35. (a) Wallis | (b) Wallace | (c) Warris |
| 36. (a) Pearson | (b) Pearston | (c) Pearstron |
| 37. (a) Rhostra | (b) Rodda | (c) Rhonda |
| 38. (a) Tailor | (b) Taylor | (c) Tail |
| 39. (a) Carter | (b) Carver | (c) Carstair |
| 40. (a) Zuiler | (b) Zweger | (c) Zueeter |
| 41. (a) Stanine | (b) Stanton | (c) Stanned |
| 42. (a) Able | (b) Abel | (c) Abbot |
| 43. (a) Travers | (b) Traverse | (c) Travart |
| 44. (a) Quintcy | (b) Quinton | (c) Quintel |
| 45. (a) Gromner | (b) Grommer | (c) Gronner |
| 46. (a) Rabbis | (b) Rabbes | (c) Rabast |
| 47. (a) Norving | (b) Norway | (c) Norwyn |
| 48. (a) Wrighton | (b) Whiton | (c) Whitton |
| 49. (a) Crabbes | (b) Crates | (c) Crabs |
| 50. (a) Zeron | (b) Zero | (c) Zerox |

| | | |
|---|---|---|
| 51. (a) Cane | (b) Caine | (c) Cayne |
| 52. (a) Rushton | (b) Tushton | (c) Riston |
| 53. (a) Noord | (b) Nourd | (c) Nord |
| 54. (a) Sarid | (b) Sarit | (c) Sarip |
| 55. (a) Constable | (b) Constabulary | (c) Constible |
| 56. (a) Farringdon | (b) Faringone | (c) Farrington |
| 57. (a) Gribble | (b) Grimble | (c) Gristle |
| 58. (a) Saul | (b) Tall | (c) Paul |
| 59. (a) Yacht | (b) Yapped | (c) Yaed |
| 60. (a) Lines | (b) Lyes | (c) Linde |
| 61. (a) Rapport | (b) Robot | (c) Redditch |
| 62. (a) Clore | (b) Clare | (c) Clair |
| 63. (a) Zeus | (b) Zude | (c) Zoo |
| 64. (a) Bable | (b) Able | (c) Abbot |
| 65. (a) Right | (b) Plight | (c) Sight |
| 66. (a) Carryon | (b) Carrion | (c) Clarion |
| 67. (a) Wavey | (b) Wacey | (c) Wackey |
| 68. (a) Ingrid | (b) Ingret | (c) Ingreed |
| 69. (a) Derry | (b) Derron | (c) Derret |
| 70. (a) Querible | (b) Queastor | (c) Quest |

## Finish

*PLEASE COMPLETE ALL THE TESTS BEFORE LOOKING AT THE ANSWERS.*

## Analytical ability

In this test we are looking at the way in which you can analyse information and draw logical conclusions. You are to use only the information given.

You may find it easier to have a piece of scrap paper when you tackle this test. There are two types of question and here are examples of both:

### Type 1

*Here you are given some information and asked to answer the question following using the facts as they have been given. Put a cross through the answer you believe to be correct. The example has been answered to show you how to proceed.*

Jean and Janet like skipping. Jane and Jean wear glasses.

Who might break her glasses while skipping? (J̶e̶a̶n̶, Janet, Jane)

### Type 2

*Here you are given a statement in bold type and four facts. You have to choose the two facts that are necessary to make the statement true. Only two facts taken together are essential. Put a cross through the letters of the two facts. The example has been done for you.*

**Hightown is north of Lowtown.**

(̶a̶) Lowtown is south of Midtown
(b) Hightown is north of Centerville
(c) Centerville is south of Midtown
(̶d̶) Midtown is south of Hightown

Here are some examples for you to try.

## Sample questions

Jim is taller than Jack. John is taller than Jim.

1. Who is tallest? (Jim, Jack, John)
2. Who is shortest? (Jim, Jack, John)

Anne and Albert like dogs. Alfred and Augusta like horses. Anne and Augusta are tall.

3. Who was the tall girl out riding? (Anne, Albert, Alfred, Augusta)

**Anville is north of Deeside.**

4. (a) Deeside is south of Beeside.
   (b) Anville is north of Beeside.
   (c) Beeside is east of Seatown.
   (d) Deeside is south-west of Seatown.

**Sam is tall and dark.**

5. (a) Sam and Paul are tall.
   (b) Paul and Percy are not dark.
   (c) Percy and Ernest are not tall.
   (d) Ernest and Sam are not fair.

*Now turn over for the answers.*

# Answers

1. John
2. Jack
3. Augusta
4. (a) and (b)
5. (a) and (d)

*Check your answers. If you have made a mistake look at the question again to see, if you can, where you went wrong.*

Now you can start the full test which begins on the next page. You have *10 minutes* to do as much as you can. You must work as accurately as you can and as fast as you can. When you are ready, start the clock and begin.

# Testing analytical ability

*Put a cross through the correct answer(s). (Remember that **two** answers are required for Type 2 questions.)*

Lowfield is bigger than Newerfield. Middlefield is bigger than Lowfield.

1. Which town is biggest? (Lowfield, Newerfield, Middlefield)

Sue and Jennifer are fair. Brian and Robyn are dark. Sue and Robyn are tall.

2. Who is fair and tall? (Sue, Jennifer, Brian, Robyn)
3. Who is tall and dark? (Sue, Jennifer, Brian, Robyn)

## Martha is playing marbles.

4. (a) Martha is in the marbles team during the summer.
   (b) Martha is in the playground.
   (c) Marbles is played in the playground in summer.
   (d) All the pupils in the playground are playing marbles.

## Adam runs faster than Stuart.

5. (a) Swithin is the champion runner.
   (b) Adam can run further than Swithin.
   (c) Adam can run as fast as Swithin.
   (d) Swithin can run faster than Stuart.

Janet, Marcus, Eric and Angela sit in this order in a row left to right. Janet changes places with Eric and then Eric changes places with Marcus.

6. Who is at the right end of the row? (Janet, Marcus, Eric, Angela)
7. Who is to the left of Eric? (Janet, Marcus, Angela)

A group of friends live in a house divided into one flat per floor. Tony is in the flat below Julie and Madeleine is in the flat above Sarah. Sarah is in the flat below Tony and Julie lives with Roger. Peter lives on the top floor.

8. Who is in the bottom flat? (Tony, Julie, Madeleine, Sarah, Peter)
9. Who else shares a flat? (Tony and Madeleine, Sarah and Peter, Tony and Peter, Madeleine and Sarah)

**Some of the school choir won book tokens.**

10. (a) The whole of Form IV won attendance awards.
    (b) Some who won a book token were also given a certificate.
    (c) The attendance awards were book tokens.
    (d) All who were given a certificate were in the choir.

James is eight years old and half as old as his brother Humphrey. Jenny is two years younger than James and the same number of years older than Mark.

11. Who is the oldest? (James, Humphrey, Jenny, Mark)
12. Who is the youngest? (James, Humphrey, Jenny, Mark)
13. How old is Mark? (1, 2, 3, 4, 5, 6, 7, 8, 9)
14. How much younger is Jenny than Humphrey? (4, 6, 7, 8, 9, 10, 12 years)

Five cars had a race. The Honda beat the Rover but couldn't overtake the Astra. The Renault failed to overtake the Granada but beat the Astra.

15. Which car came last? (Honda, Rover, Astra, Renault, Granada)
16. Which car came third? (Honda, Rover, Astra, Renault, Granada)

Jane can play the piano but not the flute while Jeremy plays the violin and the flute. Shelley plays the violin but not the piano and Josephine plays the flute but not the violin.

17. If each child plays two of the three instruments, which one is likely to be similar to Jeremy? (Shelley, Jane, Josephine)

A man drove from Appleby to Trytown. Shortly after passing through Ester he stopped for coffee at Broughton which was the halfway point on his journey.

18. Which is the longest distance? (Appleby to Ester, Ester to Trytown, Broughton to Trytown, Ester to Broughton)

**Fifty candidates sat the examination.**

19. (a) Twenty candidates answered under half the questions.
    (b) There were ten failures in the examination.
    (c) Over half the questions were answered by thirty candidates.
    (d) Forty candidates were successful.

**Onetown is north-east of Threetown.**

20. (a) Onetown is two miles north of Twotown.
    (b) Twotown is two miles west of Fourtown.
    (c) Threetown is two miles west of Twotown.
    (d) Fourtown is south-east of Onetown.

Sunday was wetter than Monday but sunnier than Saturday.

21. Which day was wettest? (Saturday, Sunday, Monday)

**Today is a Tuesday.**

22. (a) June began on a Wednesday this year.
    (b) Three days ago it was Saturday.
    (c) It is 21 June today
    (d) 22 June was on a Tuesday last year.

Six families live in a three-storey block of flats. They are numbered so that even numbers have a door on the right and odd numbers a door on the left. Numbers 1 and 2 are on the ground floor; 3 and 4 on the first floor and 5 and 6 on the top floor. The Laskeys have a door on the right and are between two families.

23. Where do the Laskeys live? (1, 2, 3, 4, 5, 6)

In the same block, the Epsons live in an even-numbered flat with the Raymonds below them. The Rowans live opposite the Laskeys and the Roses and Ewells both live opposite families with different initials.

24. Where do the Roses live? (1, 2, 3, 4, 5, 6)
25. Who lives opposite the Raymonds? (Epsons, Rowans, Laskeys, Roses, Ewells)
26. Who is over the Laskeys? (Epsons, Raymonds, Rowans, Roses, Ewells)
27. Who is at number 1? (Epsons, Raymonds, Rowans, Laskeys, Roses, Ewells)
28. Who is at number 6? (Epsons, Raymonds, Rowans, Laskeys, Roses, Ewells)

Percy Howard and his wife, Mary, and one of his twin daughters live on the corner of Apple Walk and Peartree Road. They also have two sons (Jack and Geoff) who live either side of them. Jack is married to Abigail and they live in Peartree Road. Susan shares her name with her sister-in-law who still lives at home. Stephanie is divorced from David and lives in the next town but visits her brother and his two sons in Apple Walk regularly. All the immediate family have been mentioned.

29. Who lives in Apple Walk? (David and Stephanie, Geoff and Stephanie, Geoff and Susan, Susan and Jack)
30. Who lives with Mr and Mrs Howard? (Mary, Abigail, Susan, Stephanie)
31. Who are the twins? (Mary and Susan, Susan and Stephanie, Abigail and Stephanie, Abigail and Mary)

Finish

*PLEASE COMPLETE ALL THE TESTS BEFORE LOOKING AT THE ANSWERS.*

# Marking and interpreting the tests

*PLEASE COMPLETE ALL THE TESTS BEFORE ATTEMPTING TO BEGIN MARKING.*

For each question there is one acceptable answer. In each test count one point where your answer matches the answer given in these results. At the end of each test count the number of correct marks that you have gained. This is your raw test score.

When you have found your raw score compare it with the grading tables under the answers. This is your guide for that particular test. The group which has been used to produce these comparisons is slightly above the average for the whole country. All have, or confidently expect to have, at least two GCSEs (or GCEs) at grade C or above. These grades can then be drawn on the main chart on page 65.

## Verbal reasoning: Answers

| | | | |
|---|---|---|---|
| 1. (a) | 12. (d) | 23. (c) | 34. (a) |
| 2. (b) | 13. (d) | 24. (c) | 35. (c) |
| 3. (d) | 14. (c) | 25. (c) | 36. (d) |
| 4. (c) | 15. (a) | 26. (b) | 37. (a) |
| 5. (b) | 16. (b) | 27. (d) | 38. (b) |
| 6. (a) | 17. (d) | 28. (a) | 39. (d) |
| 7. (b) | 18. (a) | 29. (a) | 40. (a) |
| 8. (c) | 19. (d) | 30. (d) | 41. (c) |
| 9. (d) | 20. (c) | 31. (a) | 42. (c) |
| 10. (a) | 21. (b) | 32. (d) | |
| 11. (c) | 22. (b) | 33. (c) | |

*Grades*

| | |
|---|---|
| A score of 30 or over | grade A |
| 26–29 | grade B |
| 23–25 | grade C |
| 19–22 | grade D |
| 15–18 | grade E |
| 14 or under | grade F |

# Numerical reasoning: Answers

| | | | |
|---|---|---|---|
| 1. (b) | 7. (a) | 13. (d) | 19. (c) |
| 2. (c) | 8. (b) | 14. (b) | 20. (d) |
| 3. (d) | 9. (d) | 15. (a) | 21. (b) |
| 4. (d) | 10. (c) | 16. (b) | |
| 5. (c) | 11. (b) | 17. (d) | |
| 6. (c) | 12. (a) | 18. (d) | |

*Grades*

| | |
|---|---|
| A score of 17 or over | grade A |
| 13–16 | grade B |
| 11–12 | grade C |
| 8–10 | grade D |
| 4– 7 | grade E |
| 3 or under | grade F |

# Perceptual reasoning: Answers

| | | | |
|---|---|---|---|
| 1. (a) | 10. (b) | 19. (c) | 28. (d) |
| 2. (c) | 11. (a) | 20. (b) | 29. (a) |
| 3. (c) | 12. (c) | 21. (d) | 30. (c) |
| 4. (a) | 13. (d) | 22. (a) | 31. (a) |
| 5. (a) | 14. (b) | 23. (d) | 32. (d) |
| 6. (c) | 15. (a) | 24. (c) | 33. (a) |
| 7. (b) | 16. (d) | 25. (b) | 34. (d) |
| 8. (d) | 17. (d) | 26. (b) | 35. (b) |
| 9. (c) | 18. (d) | 27. (c) | |

*Grades*

| | |
|---|---|
| A score of 30 or over | grade A |
| 27–29 | grade B |
| 24–26 | grade C |
| 21–23 | grade D |
| 18–20 | grade E |
| 17 or under | grade F |

# Spatial ability: Answers

| | | | |
|---|---|---|---|
| 1. N | 21. Y | 40. Y | 60. N |
| 2. N | 22. Y | 41. N | 61. N |
| 3. Y | 23. N | 42. N | 62. N |
| 4. Y | 24. N | 43. Y | 63. Y |
| 5. Y | 25. Y | 44. Y | 64. Y |
| 6. Y | 26. N | 45. N | 65. Y |
| 7. N | 27. Y | 46. N | 66. Y |
| 8. N | 28. N | 47. Y | 67. N |
| 9. Y | 29. N | 48. N | 68. Y |
| 10. N | 30. Y | 49. Y | 69. Y |
| 11. Y | 31. N | 50. N | 70. N |
| 12. N | 32. N | 51. N | 71. N |
| 13. N | 33. Y | 52. N | 72. N |
| 14. Y | 34. N | 53. N | 73. Y |
| 15. N | 35. N | 54. N | 74. N |
| 16. N | 36. Y | 55. Y | 75. N |
| 17. Y | 37. N | 56. N | |
| 18. Y | 38. N | 57. Y | |
| 19. Y | 39. Y | 58. Y | |
| 20. Y | | 59. N | |

## Grades

| | |
|---|---|
| A score of 60 or over | grade A |
| 51–59 | grade B |
| 44–50 | grade C |
| 37–43 | grade D |
| 27–36 | grade E |
| 26 or under | grade F |

# Technical ability: Answers

| | | | |
|---|---|---|---|
| 1. (c) | 10. (d) | 18. (a) | 26. (d) |
| 2. (b) | 11. (c) | 19. (a) | 27. (c) |
| 3. (c) | 12. (c) | 20. (b) | 28. (b) |
| 4. (b) | 13. (b) | 21. (c) | 29. (a) |
| 5. (b) | 14. (a) | 22. (a) | 30. (b) |
| 6. (c) | 15. (c) | 23. (a) | 31. (d) |
| 7. (a) | 16. (b) | 24. (b) | 32. (b) |
| 8. (a) | 17. (a) | 25. (c) | 33. (c) |
| 9. (a) | | | |

## *Grades*

| | |
|---|---|
| A score of 29 or over | grade A |
| 26–28 | grade B |
| 22–25 | grade C |
| 18–21 | grade D |
| 14–17 | grade E |
| 13 or under | grade F |

# Acuity skills: Answers

## Part 1

| | | | | |
|---|---|---|---|---|
| 1. 29 | 2. 80 | 3. 104 | 4. 107 | 5. 57 |
| 6. 156 | 7. 276 | 8. 392 | 9. 183 | 10. 35 |
| 11. 29 | 12. 315 | 13. 52 | 14. 871 | 15. 123 |
| 16. 79 | 17. 235 | 18. 91 | 19. 73 | 20. 5277 |
| 21. 1720 | 22. 99 | 23. 333 | 24. 121 | 25. 388 |
| 26. 225 | 27. 124 | 28. 106 | 29. 192 | 30. 758 |
| 31. 90 | 32. 96 | 33. 79 | 34. 473 | 35. 588 |

## Part 2

| | | | | |
|---|---|---|---|---|
| 1. (c) | 16. (a) | 31. (b) | 46. (c) | 61. (a) |
| 2. (c) | 17. (c) | 32. (a) | 47. (a) | 62. (c) |
| 3. (c) | 18. (a) | 33. (c) | 48. (b) | 63. (a) |
| 4. (b) | 19. (a) | 34. (b) | 49. (a) | 64. (c) |
| 5. (a) | 20. (b) | 35. (b) | 50. (b) | 65. (b) |
| 6. (c) | 21. (a) | 36. (a) | 51. (b) | 66. (b) |
| 7. (b) | 22. (a) | 37. (c) | 52. (c) | 67. (b) |
| 8. (a) | 23. (c) | 38. (c) | 53. (a) | 68. (c) |
| 9. (b) | 24. (b) | 39. (c) | 54. (a) | 69. (c) |
| 10. (a) | 25. (b) | 40. (c) | 55. (b) | 70. (b) |
| 11. (b) | 26. (b) | 41. (a) | 56. (b) | |
| 12. (c) | 27. (a) | 42. (c) | 57. (a) | |
| 13. (a) | 28. (a) | 43. (c) | 58. (c) | |
| 14. (b) | 29. (b) | 44. (a) | 59. (a) | |
| 15. (c) | 30. (c) | 45. (b) | 60. (c) | |

Add the score from Part 1 to the score from Part 2.

*Grades*

| | |
|---|---|
| A score of 74 or over | grade A |
| 66–73 | grade B |
| 53–65 | grade C |
| 40–52 | grade D |
| 32–39 | grade E |
| 31 or under | grade F |

## Analytical ability: Answers

On the questions where two answers were required, both
answers must be given correctly to score a point.

1. Middlefield
2. Sue
3. Robyn
4. (b) and (d)
5. (c) and (d)
6. Angela
7. Marcus
8. Sarah
9. Tony and
   Madeleine

10. (b) and (d)
11. Humphrey
12. Mark
13. 4
14. 10 years
15. Rover
16. Astra
17. Shelley
18. Ester to
    Trytown
19. (b) and (d)
20. (a) and (c)

21. Sunday
22. (a) and (c)
23. 4
24. 5
25. Ewells
26. Epsons
27. Ewells
28. Epsons
29. Geoff and
    Susan
30. Susan
31. Susan and
    Stephanie

*Grades*

| | |
|---|---|
| A score of 23 or over | grade A |
| 20–22 | grade B |
| 16–19 | grade C |
| 11–15 | grade D |
| 8–10 | grade E |
| 7 or under | grade F |

# Your abilities profile chart

Transfer your grades from pages 60 to 64 on to this chart.

| Verbal reasoning | Numerical reasoning | Perceptual reasoning | Spatial ability | Technical ability | Acuity skills | Analytical ability |
|---|---|---|---|---|---|---|
| A | A | A | A | A | A | A |
| B | B | B | B | B | B | B |
| C | C | C | C | C | C | C |
| D | D | D | D | D | D | D |
| E | E | E | E | E | E | E |
| F | F | F | F | F | F | F |
| Verbal reasoning | Numerical reasoning | Perceptual reasoning | Spatial ability | Technical ability | Acuity skills | Analytical ability |

## Interpreting your ability results

The profile graph of your ability test results tells you two different things. First it gives you an idea of the general level of your abilities and second, an idea of your particular strengths and weaknesses.

The grades are based on a sample of people, most of whom had gained some kind of academic qualification ranging from two or three GCSEs, grade C upwards.

Bearing this in mind, think first about how these results and your profile match your attainments and experience. Do they reflect the results and qualifications you have already obtained? Are the strengths and weaknesses as you expected?

These types of test can have drawbacks. Timing has to be accurate and variations in your timing can affect your scores. Similarly, if you are timing yourself and spent a disproportionate amount of time watching the clock to make sure that you stopped on time you may not have done yourself justice.

Your test score may also vary slightly if you are feeling particularly tired or a little panicky. And, finally, this type of test does tend to penalise the slow but accurate worker who checks answers as he or she progresses. This is because no account is taken of the number of correct answers versus the number of incorrect ones.

## Level of results

When you look at the overall level of the results you should be able to compare it with your results in examinations and other tests.

If your results are generally below average, you are unlikely to do well in examinations, particularly against the clock. You may well find that practical subjects suit you better.

If your results are generally around the average, you probably did quite well at school but may not have taken many further qualifications of an academic nature.

If your results are generally above average, you are likely to do well in most areas and you may well be thinking of careers which involve further study and qualifications.

The level of your results gives you an indication of the ease with which you can tackle problems in these areas. A very determined and conscientious individual can sometimes achieve more than the results suggest. Similarly, a less well-disciplined individual may under-achieve generally. However, the level of your results on these tests should be roughly in line with your experience. If there is virtually no connection between the two, you may well be the one person in a thousand for whom these tests do not completely work and you would be wise to seek advice from a professional careers counsellor.

# Pattern of results

There are two broad types of test and you should look first at the distinction between the two.

If you have done better on the verbal, numerical, perceptual and analytical tests you are likely to be more academically biased and will generally do well in areas where theoretical knowledge and an ability to 'see' the underlying structure are most valuable. These areas include professional jobs such as librarian, accountant or research scientist.

If, on the other hand, you did better on the technical, spacial and acuity tests you are more likely to do well in areas which primarily use 'applied' knowledge, such as engineering, applied sciences, and areas of management which rely on ability and experience.

For many people, however, there is no clear distinction between these two broad groups and you will need to look further at the interpretations.

There are many possible results but we will concentrate on the seven individual strengths and the 21 paired combinations.

Look at your strongest score(s) to find out which profile is most representative of your underlying abilities.

# Individual strengths

*Verbal ability*
This strength is the ability to reason with words. This is often connected with literary careers but is also a very important attribute in those careers which involve the ability to find the right word at the right time. This may be the spoken word or the written word and is the single most useful strength in any kind of academic study.

This strength is most noticeable in a career as an author, a copywriter, a poet, a salesperson, a teacher, a linguist or a personnel director.

*Numerical ability*
This ability is similar to, but not the same as, mathematical ability. It is the ability to 'think' in numbers rather than the

ability to manipulate them. There are comparatively few careers which require numerical ability alone; it is more often mixed with other abilities. Careers which are heavily dependent upon this ability include those as an auditor, a wage clerk, a bank teller. Many areas of finance depend on it too.

## Perceptual ability

This ability requires you to 'see' abstract information and to make sense of it. It is one of the cornerstones of scientific thinking. The stages of building concepts, discovery and proving theories all rely heavily on this aptitude. Thus it is a key to most scientific-based careers, including those as a research scientist, a laboratory technician, a veterinary surgeon, a dietician, a hospital technician and similar science-based personnel at all levels.

## Spatial ability

This is the ability which enables you to visualise a solid three-dimensional object when given limited two-dimensional information. It is the cornerstone of understanding technical drawings, layout and the relationships between objects in space and as such it will be used heavily by draughtsmen, creative artists, hairdressers, photographers and designers.

## Technical ability

This test reveals the naturalness with which you cope with the world around you. It has more to do with your basic reaction to a practical problem than your learnt response. You do not have to be 'practical' but you probably will be if you score highly on this test. It is of particular use in careers for mechanics, lathe operators, maintenance personnel and assembly workers. It is also one of the most important abilities in the range of skills needed by engineers.

## Acuity skills

This is the ability to do routine tasks quickly and with great accuracy. It is one of the few aptitudes that can increase noticeably with practice but the results will give a realistic guide as to how 'easy' you find this kind of task compared with others.

It is of particular use in many clerical areas such as filing, typing and computer operating. It is also of importance in areas such as quality inspection.

*Analytical ability*

This is the ability to make logical, factual connections and to impose a structure on what sometimes appears to be chaotic information. It reflects the ability to think quickly, confining yourself to the facts only, to solve problems and to deal with new ideas.

It is frequently combined with other aptitudes to indicate the direction in which this ability to think is going to be used. The particular test in this book asks verbal questions as this is the most common way in which this ability is actually used at work. Reasonable verbal ability is required as well as 'pure' analytical ability.

It is of particular importance in careers such as computer programmer, researcher or analyst.

## Two main factor combinations

It is quite unusual to have one single strong ability and indeed, as can be seen from the examples, there are comparatively few careers which require just one. It is better to look at the major abilities and see where combinations of these could lead.

*Verbal/Numerical* Here the ability to reason equally well in words and numbers is the key for careers which would include commercial managers, senior administrators, insurance agents and head teachers.

*Verbal/Perceptual* A descriptive scientist is the most helpful single description here but the ability is also found in areas of science which are not quite so heavily dependent on numerical ability. For instance, biologists and geographers would have this combination together with authors of scientific books and scientific journalists.

*Verbal/Spatial* This combination contains both the ability to use words and the ability to see three-dimensionally. This could be most useful for photojournalists, editors, creative directors, design consultants and publishers.

*Verbal/Technical* This area is similar to verbal/perceptual but bases understanding on the technical or applied side of science rather than the more theoretical issues, hence technical writers, engineering representatives and patents agents would find this combination valuable.

*Verbal/Acuity* This is the area where you are primarily dealing with words and having to do so with great accuracy and speed. Many 'office'-type tasks fall into this category and in particular those of legal executives, word processor operators, translators, proof readers, personnel assistants and secretaries would all be expected to have this combination as a strength.

*Verbal/Analytical* This combination is frequently found in people working at the professional end of a scale where the ability to understand what lies beneath the surface as well as the ability to describe it are needed. In particular, barristers, science journal editors, psychologists, philosophers and management consultants frequently have these strengths.

*Numerical/Perceptual* These strengths are particularly valuable for the 'harder' scientific approaches, especially at the higher levels. Examples in this area would include analytical chemists, metallurgists, astronomers, nuclear physicists.

*Numerical/Spatial* This is a comparatively unusual combination which links the ability to visualise with a 'feel' for numbers. Examples of suitable careers, however, would include surveying, architecture and art dealing.

*Numerical/Technical* This is a common combination in the applied science and technical fields. Design engineers, physicists, tool makers and structural engineers need this combination.

*Numerical/Acuity* The dual strengths are most valuable in many areas of finance. Insurance actuaries, accounts clerks, statisticians (producers) and information technologists (producers of information) need these strengths.

*Numerical/Analytical*   The emphasis changes slightly on to the underlying understanding of the numerical activities and the ability to describe these processes and is best illustrated by careers such as a statistician (analyst), stock broker, mathematician, systems analyst, information technologist (analytical) and psychometrician.

*Perceptual/Spatial*   This is a slightly unusual mixture combining scientific understanding with the ability to visualise in three dimensions and is probably best identified by careers such as medical photography, biological illustration and radiography.

*Perceptual/Technical*   This is the combination that provides both an understanding of the scientific principle together with the application of the technical. It is found in many areas of technology but a few slightly more unusual ones would include careers as a hospital physicist, laboratory technician, heating and ventilation technician and inventor.

*Perceptual/Acuity*   Activities combining these two particular strengths are more specialist, requiring an understanding in science (particularly the softer sciences) and greater attention to detail. Careers such as pharmacy technician, pathology technician and medical administrator could be included here.

*Perceptual/Analytical*   This is really a very general combination which includes virtually all academic scientists and areas where the emphasis is on the underlying reasoning and the understanding of that reasoning, and the communication of that understanding, rather than necessarily having to apply it in a particular direction.

*Spatial/Technical*   Careers here would include electronics engineering, lithographic printing, technical illustration and orthodontics.

*Spatial/Acuity*   In this combination the visual ability together with an 'eye' for detail would benefit map tracers, print makers, animators and tilers.

*Spatial/Analytical*   A fairly unusual combination of abilities linking the visual with the more 'academic' approach but

careers in this area could include art history, graphic pro-
gramme design and economics.

*Technical/Acuity*   There are many 'technician' posts requiring
great accuracy that would normally fall in this category. Some
of the slightly more unusual ones are photographic technician,
patents exminer, architectural draughtsman and undertaker.

*Technical/Analytical*   This is the combination that produces
process engineers, material scientists, information technologists (technical) and quality controllers. It combines the ability
to understand what happens with the ability to provide the
abstract logic of why it happens.

*Acuity/Analytical*   This is a most unusual combination and
mixes the ability to analyse and to think logically with an
attention to detail normally found in the more clerical tasks.
Some examples of the combination, however, would be
marketing analyst, compensation and benefits adviser, historian. Together they also provide the kind of discipline often
needed in academic research – particularly until one 'qualifies'!

There are, of course, other combinations of three or more
strengths and these would need to be looked at carefully. By
doing a little of your own combining and by using the Career
Index in Chapter 6 it is possible to find a career which tends to
suit your abilities best.

We must emphasise, however, that abilities are not all. You
do need to be both interested in, and the kind of person who
will fit best in, the kind of environment in which the particular
type of job takes place. Your abilities are only one small part of
your overall suitability for a career.

It is now time to move on to look at personality and
motivation and to understand what indications they can give
you of your most suitable natural career choice.

If you have abilities at a fairly even level, it is most important
that you pay particular attention to personality and motivation. You are not a specialist and require a career with variety.
What will make the difference between a routine job and a
successful career for you will be how well the aspects other
than ability suit you.

## Chapter 3
# Personality: What Are My Hidden Strengths?

You need to understand your personality if you are to be happy at work. It is fashionable at the moment for employers to equate happiness at work with effectiveness. It makes sense: if you are discontented you are unlikely to do your best work. You may even find yourself unwell for no apparent reason! Employers want people who are suited to the job.

This has not always been so. For example, the Victorian factory owner did not have to pay as much attention to the feelings of his workers as do today's employers. Where there is ample labour and a willingness to work because work is seen as a way to escape from hardship, employers are simply looking for 'pairs of hands' or technical skills. But as our idea of what we mean by 'produce' moves into careers where personal flair, originality and interpersonal skills are demanded, the picture changes.

We often use words such as lively, exuberant or cheerful to describe personality. Increasingly, work which does not require 'personality' is replaced by machines. But many jobs which appear monotonous or routine are still undertaken by people because of the particular skills required. These may be tasks on a production line where experience of assessing defects in quality goods is essential (cars are still 'eyeballed' before being sent to the showroom). Divers as well as astronauts have to contend with long periods of boredom and routine in conditions where movement and expression are obviously seriously restricted. In these and other highly skilled jobs, a particular kind of personality is required and employers have learned to select people who can endure calmly and remain alert in particular conditions.

So it is essential that your personality should be taken into account. The happier you are at work the better it is likely to be for you, first because you will feel that you are achieving and second, for the business or industry you are in because, frankly, you are likely to contribute more. Additionally, labour is an expensive resource these days, and your employer will have less cost associated with rehiring, retraining, strikes, stoppage or wastage if you are happy.

There are lots of theories as to what personality consists of. Some words associated with personality which have passed into common usage, eg 'id', 'super-ego', 'libido', are not very useful when it comes to the practicalities of different types of work.

You may well ask whether it is worth measuring personality. The question is often asked more directly: Is personality measurable? Our personality as it expresses itself in moods and other behaviour is infinitely variable; we all seem to have the potential at different times to be able to take on different types of personality. Sometimes we are not even acting; we become angry or obstinate or considerate or emotional or generous or frightened or quiet or noisy even though we do not normally act in this way. It is almost as though we can change ourselves, like a chameleon, to fit the conditions or the demands that are placed upon us.

It is our experience that most of us can act 'out of character' for a short time. We might 'go along with' situations in which we are unhappy, or even dislike, for the sake of convenience. But our 'normal' personality always seems to reassert itself.

This is not to say that we do not ever change. We change as a result of experience and through self-awareness. Shyness has been shown by researchers to change sometimes considerably as a person gets older. Personality changes can also come about through self-awareness or self-assurance, simply through a decision to change an aspect of yourself. People often do this by working hard to change something about themselves they do not like. You don't like public speaking? Take a public speaking course and keep on practising and you will find that it becomes second nature. You feel left out at parties? Rehearse a number of jokes before you go to your next party and you will find that you are becoming the life and soul. Afraid of strangers? An analyst or counsellor will be able to help you find out why this is 'blocking' your personality.

What, then, is your 'normal' personality? There is no doubt that you have a personality which is recognisable and familiar to the people who know you. You behave and react in characteristic ways. This is why people make relationships with you; it is why you are recognised by old friends and renew friendships even after many years in which you may have gone a completely different way from someone you grew up with. People say, 'You haven't changed a bit.'

It is because people have identifiable and consistent personality characteristics that it is sensible to relate these to a job. But bear in mind that as your own personality grows and changes you may need a career which does not stifle you. Some careers are like cul-de-sacs: they can be very comfortable and rewarding if they are going to suit you all your working life, but they can become a trap if you would prefer to be working along a different career path.

For example, your personality attributes of factual-mindedness may have led you to pass examinations and obtain a career as a technical expert – perhaps you are now a technician or scientist, or maybe you have become a statistician or computer engineer. But then you become aware that you are not getting the opportunities you would like to meet other people in your work. You may decide you have some leadership qualities and want to get into some form of management. Are there opportunities in the career you have chosen at the outset to broaden yourself and to find new challenges or will you have to start all over again? Although many people nowadays do take up second careers, and no doubt this book will be of help to such people, it is often a painful and difficult reorientation. We would prefer your career to flow naturally onwards and upwards rather than be filled with starts, stops and reversals.

Are you still unsure about the importance of personality upon career? You won't mind then if the surgeon has a 'flip', cheery or casual approach as he picks up his scalpel! Nor will you mind, as you board your plane taking you to your holiday in Majorca, that the technician fixing the engine is 'laid back'. And if you are an employer you will see no disadvantage in taking on as salespeople those who are either grouchy or too afraid to say boo to a goose. In our work connected with vocational guidance we have met thousands of people with whom we have discussed careers and we have become increasingly convinced of the folly or pursuing a career which is inconsistent with a person's type of personality. Too often we have seen people strive to achieve something for which they did not have the necessary characteristics and then feel a failure as a result. This is unnecessary. It is much better to enjoy doing what suits you. Here again, a little self-awareness helps. Stubbornness and determination can be excellent qualities and will help you achieve a task but taken too far these same qualities can turn into obstinacy and foolhardiness. It is far more sensible, if you find a career stressful, to lick your wounds and try something that suits you better. You should not stick at it just for the money or because you are trying to prove something to yourself.

Whatever your age now, your personality will have some stabilised traits and it is these that we can apply to different kinds of work. However, you need to bear in mind that your pesonality may appear to grow or change as you become more aware of your potential. Even doing the personality questionnaire can help you to increase your self-awareness so that you may well see yourself differently from the person you were before! But don't expect to change very radically or quickly and don't go into a career which manifestly does not fit your characteristics simply because you admire people who are different from yourself.

Will the personality test tell you anything you do not already know about yourself? Probably not; but there is little doubt that you know yourself better than anybody else does. At the same time you may not know how to relate your personality to different jobs. The personality test will help you to structure your ideas about your personality in useful ways. It will not measure all of your personality and it is not intended to deal with those aspects which are more relevant to your personal and private life. Here we are concerned with how your personality relates you to one type of work rather than another. Nobody has a multi-potential personality and just as personality enables us to achieve in some ways, it limits what we may achieve in others.

Let us take the case of the sales personality which most people would agree has distinct characteristics. These are in contrast to many of the characteristics required in other careers such as, for example, that of scientific researcher. For the salesman interpersonal skills come first and foremost, with technical abilities usually a secondary requirement. It is the reverse for the researcher: where acquired skill and knowledge characterise the jobs technical ability is vital. Here, paradoxically, a strange phenomenon may occur: salesmen often admire education and wish they had a quieter, more academic disposition; conversely researchers sometimes feel that career development is inhibited, not by exam prowess, but by lack of a more sociable and confident nature. Obviously this is not always the case, but we have witnessed it often enough to know that a great many people admire characteristics in others that they do not have themselves. However, it is wise to concentrate on those continuing aspects of our personality however much we might want to change ourselves. Not to do so is as profitless as trying to walk through a low doorway without bending one's head or, not being a swimmer, diving straight into the deep end!

## The personality tests

It is easier to spot what ability tests are trying to get at than it is with the tests of personality. In fact you may feel that the personality tests are trying to catch you out. This is not really the case! If you try to second guess the question or reply in a way that you know is not true for you the only person you will be catching out is yourself. The aim is for you to see certain aspects of your personality as clearly as possible. You can then relate the way your personality typically expresses itself to different types of work.

As you take these tests it may seem to you that you are answering one way now but might feel differently tomorrow and therefore respond in a completely different way. Feelings do change from day to day but they are not likely to change sufficiently to alter the results significantly.

When you respond to the personality tests it is best to think of yourself as you are now. Do not pretend that you are somebody else and do not think of yourself as you would like to be or think perhaps you could be. As a matter of fact, nearly everybody thinks that there is a better person within them trying to get out and that if only they were given the right chance then that person would emerge. In fact it is true, because no one is ever likely to be completely self-satisfied and therefore we are all trying to change ourselves in small ways. Even though the intent of these tests is to discover the real you, it is going to be most useful if you respond to the tests in a way that is a true statement about you, your feelings and your behaviour. In this way we will be able to draw some practical conclusions.

If you really are in two minds as to how you should take a test then it is probably best to take it twice. First of all take it as you feel you actually are now and see how your results come out. Then take it again, bearing in mind the personality characteristics you truly believe you would like to have. You will then be able to see whether you would really like the type of work done by people with the characteristics you admire. You can do this for interest rather than for any practical purpose. However, if you are confused at the end of all the tests about whether you have the personality to take on the career which appeals to you or whether you can change your personality in ways that you think you would like, then you had better see a vocational guidance counsellor.

## Instructions

In all the personality tests you are asked to say whether you agree or disagree with various statements. Remember that there are no right or wrong answers. The answers you give will reflect your general thoughts and feelings. It is often difficult to say clearly whether you agree or not but just put down what tends to be true for you.

In completing the personality tests do not think about careers at all. Just think about yourself and your behaviour in all aspects of your life. You should circle the answer which agrees with the way you normally feel. Although it is difficult to be absolutely certain about some of the statements, do not spend too long making up your mind. It is generally just as good to give a quick response as to spend a long time mulling over the possibilities.

Do not leave any questions unanswered. The example below has been done for you.

*Example:*
When I sleep I very rarely dream | I | **YES** (NO) | G |

If you circle NO, this indicates that you do in fact dream.

Ignore the letters on each side of YES and NO: these will be explained later. Now carry on with Part 1 of the questionnaire.

# The personality questionnaire

S-F, C-L,
P-A, I-G

*Part 1*

| | | | | |
|---|---|---|---|---|
| 1. I generally like to work by myself in my own way | I | **YES** | NO | G |
| 2. I quickly get to know new people | A | YES | NO | P |
| 3. Little mistakes I have made sometimes worry me | S | YES | NO | F |
| 4. I often do things without thinking | L | YES | NO | C |
| 5. I cannot forget my problems very easily | S | YES | NO | F |
| 6. I have no difficulty in settling down to work on something difficult | C | YES | NO | L |
| 7. Even if everyone else disagrees I say what I think | A | YES | NO | P |
| 8. I prefer someone else to be the leader | P | YES | NO | A |
| 9. I like to do the same thing as my friends | G | YES | NO | I |
| 10. I try hard to make sure I do not hurt another person's feelings | S | YES | NO | F |
| 11. I like to do a thing carefully to make sure it is done correctly even if it means giving up something else | C | YES | NO | L |
| 12. Many things I read about in books and newspapers are sad | S | YES | NO | F |
| 13. I frequently find it difficult to admit that I may be wrong | F | YES | NO | S |

| | | | | |
|---|---|---|---|---|
| 14. | I usually take life as it comes | C | (YES) NO | L |
| 15. | I think I work best in a team | G | YES (NO) | I |
| 16. | I prefer to be at home rather than go to parties | P | (YES) NO | A |
| 17. | I am always interested in the latest fashions | L | YES (NO) | C |
| 18. | There is too much pain and misery in this world | S | YES (NO) | F |
| 19. | I hate to be sitting down for too long | L | YES (NO) | C |
| 20. | I am quick to try exciting new things | L | (YES) NO | C |
| 21. | I am confident in most situations | F | YES (NO) | S |
| 22. | I do not get as easily upset by things as other people | F | YES (NO) | S |
| 23. | I support my friends no matter what | G | YES (NO) | I |
| 24. | I sometimes worry about what others think of me | P | (YES) NO | A |
| 25. | I nearly always have something to say in a discussion | A | (YES) NO | P |
| 26. | I sometimes lie awake thinking about little things that have not gone quite right | S | (YES) NO | F |
| 27. | I do not mind telling others about my private feelings | G | YES (NO) | I |
| 28. | I do not know what I would do without my friends | G | YES (NO) | I |
| 29. | I often do things without informing others | I | (YES) NO | G |

| | | | | |
|---|---|---|---|---|
| 30. | I like to win people round to my way of thinking | A | **YES** NO | R |
| 31. | I often get sidetracked while doing something | L | **YES** NO | C |
| 32. | After I have made a decision I am likely to change my mind | L | **YES** NO | C |
| 33. | I like to help people get to know each other | A | YES **NO** | P |
| 34. | The fun of having a secret is being able to pass it on | G | YES **NO** | I |
| 35. | I find it difficult to make a decision if it is going to upset someone | S | **YES** NO | F |
| 36. | I prefer to listen than to talk | R | **YES** NO | A |
| 37. | I soon make it up after an argument | A | YES **NO** | P |
| 38. | I am more or less happy with myself as I am | C | YES **NO** | L |
| 39. | I like people to ask me before borrowing my things | I | **YES** NO | G |
| 40. | I like to share my problems with my friends | G | YES **NO** | I |

## Part 2

In Part 2 of the questionnaire you have to think about how others might describe you. In doing this, try not to be either modest or immodest: your answers should reflect truthfully notions of the feelings you suspect that others have of you. (If you ask these questions directly of friends or family, make sure you get a truthful and not a diplomatic answer and ask yourself also how biased those people might be.)

Part 2 consists of a list of words or phrases which people may use to describe you. You are to ask yourself whether people in general would use this word or phrase to describe you. Again, you are asked to circle one of the answers – **YES** or **NO** – as you did in Part 1. Again, take no notice of the letters at this stage; their purpose will be explained later. Now complete Part 2 of the personality questionnaire.

People would generally describe me as:

| | | | | |
|---|---|---|---|---|
| 1. Company-seeking | G | YES | **NO** | I |
| 2. Self-determining | I | YES | **NO** | G |
| 3. Relaxed | C | YES | **NO** | L |
| 4. Ostentatious | A | **YES** | NO | P |
| 5. Retiring | P | **YES** | NO | A |
| 6. Sentimental | S | **YES** | NO | F |
| 7. Conforming | G | YES | NO | I |
| 8. Confident | A | YES | **NO** | R |
| 9. Impatient | L | YES | **NO** | C |
| 10. Animated | L | YES | **NO** | C |
| 11. Hearty | A | YES | **NO** | P |
| 12. A dissenter | I | YES | **NO** | G |
| 13. One of the crowd | G | YES | **NO** | I |
| 14. Sensitive | S | YES | **NO** | F |
| 15. Willing to accept others' advice | G | YES | **NO** | I |
| 16. Effusive | A | **YES** | NO | P |
| 17. Shy | P | **YES** | NO | A |
| 18. Influenced by friends | G | YES | **NO** | I |
| 19. Realistic | F | YES | **NO** | S |
| 20. Highly strung | L | **YES** | NO | C |
| 21. Unfeeling | F | **YES** | NO | S |
| 22. Overmodest | P | YES | **NO** | A |

83

| | | | | |
|---|---|---|---|---|
| 23. Impulsive | L | **YES** | (NO) | C |
| 24. Soft-hearted | S | **YES** | (NO) | F |
| 25. Shocking | L | **YES** | (NO) | C |
| 26. Go your own way | I | (YES) | NO | G |
| 27. Tranquil | C | (YES) | NO | L |
| 28. Blunt | F | **YES** | (NO) | S |
| 29. Dreamy | S | **YES** | (NO) | F |
| 30. Moderate | C | (YES) | NO | L |
| 31. Stand on your own feet | I | (YES) | NO | G |
| 32. Factual | F | (YES) | NO | S |
| 33. Bashful | P | **YES** | (NO) | A |
| 34. Keeps 'open-house' | A | **YES** | (NO) | P |
| 35. Unruffled | C | (YES) | NO | L |
| 36. Thin-skinned | S | (YES) | NO | F |
| 37. Placid | C | (YES) | NO | L |
| 38. Objective | F | (YES) | NO | S |
| 39. Nervous | P | **YES** | (NO) | A |
| 40. A 'loner' | I | (YES) | NO | G |

## How to mark the test of personality (the FLAG test)

The letters beside the words 'yes' and 'no' were deliberately changed around and put in different columns in order to prevent you from perceiving what the test was getting at. Of course, you can quickly 'see through' the test if you want to because it is hard not to be conscious that the items seem related to each other in the same way. At the same time, mixing up the questions and changing the answers around in this way is likely to keep you thinking; it 'keeps you on your toes' and will therefore produce a truer assessment of your personality, which is what we want.

To mark the test, start with Part 1 and count up the number of times you have circled either 'yes' or 'no' by the letter F. This will give you an F score. Enter this in the table below. Do the same with the letters L, A and G.

Repeat this with Part 2. You can then add both parts for each four letters so that for each letter you get a total out of 20.

In order to check that you have added up your score correctly, take each letter in turn and add the score you have obtained for that letter to the number of times you circled the letter that goes with it. You can see that S goes with F, C goes with L, P goes with A and I goes with G. In each part the score for each pair of letters should make 10. The maximum score in Part 1 is 10 and in Part 2 is 10.

Each of your scores relates to a different aspect of personality. They can be dealt with as a whole and indeed they should be because your personality also acts with all its parts. However, for the purpose of understanding your personality it will be useful to look at the four aspects separately.

## Personality test results

| Part 1 | + | Part 2 | = | Total |
|---|---|---|---|---|
| F ( 7 ) / 10 | + | F ( 5 ) / 10 | = | 12 / 20 |
| L ( 7 ) / 10 | + | L ( ) / 10 | = | 9 / 20 |
| A ( ) / 10 | + | A ( 2 ) / 10 | = | 9 / 20 |
| G ( 3 ) / 10 | + | G ( 4 ) / 10 | = | 7 / 20 |

## What difference does it make to my career if I am more or less factual or sensitive?

You can be both factual and sensitive in the way that these descriptions are used in everyday language but in this personality test these words have particular meanings; a person may like to work with factual information, for example, but still have feelings! Therefore it is important to understand what these words mean as far as the test is concerned.

## The characteristics of F

The F scale gives you an idea of how much attention you pay to feelings and whether you will want to deal with them in a work situation. Many people think that dealing with feelings, which often involves understanding and consideration of other people's point of view, prevents a job from getting done. If you hold this view then feelings will be a distraction and you will want to get on and accomplish a task with the minimum possible fuss.

The higher your score on the F scale, the more likely it is that you have a realistic, down-to-earth, no-nonsense approach to life. You probably like to deal with factual problems which require a logical approach so that you 'know where you are'. You like to see issues as clear and outcomes as certainties. Probably you will not like vagaries and jobs which are incomplete; you like order and systems.

The positive aspect of the factual personality is the ability to boil down all sorts of issues in a clear way. Your objectivity allows you to get somewhere and make progress. You are practical and can achieve definite results. Keeping yourself detached allows you to be analytical and often perceptive.

The disadvantage of being factual is that you can have difficulty with issues of a more emotional kind which cannot be easily classified. You may as a result prefer to be in an environment where emotional issues do not 'contaminate' the problem that you are dealing with. Your austere and logical approach pays full attention to the intellectual, but at the expense of losing out on the emotional side of things. You may be able to see what is in front of you or understand with your mind but you will be less able to feel whether issues are right or wrong because they cannot be objectively demonstrated.

If you are high on the F scale you will probably be drawn towards careers in which you can work with facts, information, objects or equipment. You may like working with people but it is the end product or job itself which appeals to you.

## The characteristics of S

If you have a low score on the F scale then you are tending much more towards being sensitive. You will be keenly aware of what is said to you and about you and the way things are said will grab your attention. You will probably feel far less involved with things than about people. Logic and order will appeal to you much less than expression.

If you are very low on the F scale you will often have the ability to see both sides of an argument. You will be able to see how important an emotional issue may be. Emotional reasons for making decisions will be of more value to you than objective or legal reasons.

The disadvantage of being sensitive is that you can sometimes respond too strongly to your sense of injustice. Do you take things too personally? If you do, you might slow other people down if they haven't realised what is bothering you. Maybe you are a bit dreamy and maybe you are impractical.

If you tend more towards the sensitive end of the scale then you may well feel frustrated if your work gives you no opportunity to use your intuition. In common with people of an artistic bent you can sometimes feel discouraged or burdened by the feelings you have but out of the ferment can arise creative expression. This might find fulfilment within the arts themselves or an arts-related environment. Alternatively, you may find that your sensitivity does give you an understanding into other people's problems.

As a rough guide you can compare your own score on the F scale with those of other occupations. Remember that the examples given below also have three other aspects of personality which we are not dealing with here, so you may not be able to identify completely with any of the occupations.

Nonetheless, you can ask yourself what characteristics you have which are like those found in the occupations below. Simply mark your own score with a cross on the scale.

*F Scale*

S ┤├ F

1 2 3 4 5 6 7 8 9 10 11 12 13 14 15 16 17 18 19 20

**sensitive**                                                        **factual**

| | |
|---|---|
| artist | barrister |
| author (literary) | cameraman |
| dancer | customs officer |
| florist | diver |
| music therapist | estate agent |
| nursery nurse | mechanic |
| speech and drama teacher | prison officer |
| teacher | systems analyst |
| veterinary nurse | technician |
| window dresser | traffic warden |

## Are you a calm or a lively personality?

Whichever end of the scale you are you can get very frustrated in a job which does not correspond with this aspect of your temperament. If you are in the middle on the scale you might be able to 'bend' one way or the other to some extent, but it is difficult for you to act out of character for very long in a career which strongly requires one characteristic rather than the other.

## The characteristics of L

The lively person tends to react quickly to situations and to people. If you are like this, you will prefer things to be fast-moving; you enjoy change and variety. You may be spontaneous and make decisions 'off the top of your head'. If you are extreme, you will prefer to have many interests and you might have something of a 'butterfly mind'.

There are many positive aspects of being lively. First, you

can be very good company because you are amusing. You latch on to ideas quickly. You might almost be bubbly and effervescent. Your enthusiasm can be contagious. You want to get on and do things, and you will probably work best in a lively and frenetic career where everything is happening at once. Activities connected with the media and entertainment could interest you because of the constant variety.

A negative aspect of this personality is that you might find it difficult to finish something you have started. In fact, you sometimes have too many interests and fail to see things through to their conclusion. Because your interests are often superficial, people who are more serious or permanent might distrust you. You can also be a poor organiser. How many times are you late for appointments? In spite of this, you can probably avoid criticism through personal flair.

## The characteristics of C

If you are on the lower end of the scale and are therefore of a calm temperament, you will probably have a consistent and dependable disposition. Do you ever get ruffled by anything? – Probably not. If you do, you probably wait for things to sort themselves out rather than interfere or make a scene.

The good thing about being calm is that you can act as a firm anchor when others begin to panic. You may often save the day because your unhurried and deliberate approach wins through. People will depend on you and admire you. For example, lots of men will smoke pipes in order to try to be like you! You will be good in a job where steadiness is required since you plan your work carefully and get it done properly as well as on time.

On the minus side, a certain amount of dullness may be attributed to you. This is unfair, of course, but you may have to admit that sometimes you are a bit predictable. Do you really have to weigh matters up so carefully? And at times you seem so self-assured as to be almost pompous or smug. However, we need you since without your steady hand on the tiller, where would we all be?

You can see that in some careers the work is carried out in

an apparently immediately, impulsive and spontaneous way, and reactions have to be to the immediate subject of interest. There is sometimes a good deal of apparent pressure in such careers; this keeps people highly charged or keeps their adrenalin flowing. Alternatively, there are other careers much more suited to the placid and easy-going disposition.

Mark your own score with a cross on the L scale and see if you can identify with any of the careers which exemplify this characteristic. Bear in mind that in the examples given below other characteristics may also be required.

*L Scale*

C | | | | | | | | | | | | | | | | | | | | | L

1 2 3 4 5 6 7 8 9 10 11 12 (13) 14 (15) 16 17 18 19 20

calm                                                                lively

| | |
|---|---|
| administrator | advertising executive |
| ambulance crew | bar person |
| art therapist | conference executive |
| doctor | dancer |
| draughtsman | demonstrator |
| ergonomist | direct sales agent |
| fireman | dresser |
| guard | hairdresser |
| librarian | marketing assistant |
| lighting technician | masseur/masseuse |
| osteopath | model |
| police officer | public relations assistant |
| restorer | retail assistant |
| scientist | window dresser |
| secretary | |
| surgeon | |
| theatre administrator | |
| work study officer | |

## Will I need to be aggressive to do well in my career?

The answer to this question depends on what you mean by 'well': if you mean material success, the answer is probably yes.

If you mean that you also want to have authority and influence over others, the answer is also likely to be yes. But the word 'well' can also have other meanings if you value contentment, peace of mind or co-operation rather than conflict. It will be obvious to you that some careers require a more 'pushy' approach than others. This scale is about how active and determined you are likely to be in going out into the world and getting what you want.

## The characteristics of A

A person who is high on the A scale has an aggressive or bullish approach, and as many women can get high scores on this scale as men. Such characteristics are not generally associated with feminity: aggression has of course to do with dominance and Western society has hitherto assumed that women play a largely subordinate role. This need not necessarily be the case and attitudes towards the role of females are changing – probably because there is so much evidence around these days that women can be excellent leaders! Anthropologists have found plenty of evidence of female-dominated societies, so male dominance can in no way be regarded as an unchangeable biological characteristic.

The aggressive scale describes someone who is 'go-getting'. If you are like this, you will go out and get what you want rather than wait for it to come to you. You can be impatient at times. You will show confidence in yourself or at least such a strong need to achieve that you will overcome barriers.

You may think that the good aspect of having some aggression is that there has to be someone to organise others. You probably welcome change too. Others may look to you for leadership, recognising your willingness to push ahead and perhaps even take risks. You are not easily put off and might be able to bluff your way out when you are in a tight corner. You may be able to make money or make things happen.

On the negative side, you will often hurt others' feelings. You charge forward so much that you can be like a bull in a china shop. You may not even realise the trail of misery and hurt feelings that you have left in your wake. Getting up and doing obviously has consequences for other people. However, you may feel that it is their own fault if they get in the way. You will find people easy to deal with even if you do have to manipulate them a bit or perhaps tell them only what they need to know. You will probably be drawn to careers which give you power and influence.

## The characteristics of P

If you are of a passive disposition, you will have the ability to work in a structured way and pay attention to detail. You have a strong stoical streak and can put up with things when others would complain or rebel. You are good in the type of career in which you are behind the scenes. You will try hard to please and others will include you in their activities because they find your conscientiousness and reliability valuable.

The drawback of being too passive is that you may have difficulty in actually communicating your own needs to others. You put up with things because you fail to put yourself across. You will avoid making a fuss and of course if you resent being unappreciated it really is your own fault. However, you can get embarrassed so perhaps it is better to stay out of the limelight. You've got doubts about your self-confidence and you may not be able to step out of the boundaries of what others expect of you as well as the limits you have imposed upon yourself.

Mark your score with an X on the A scale below. Again, the careers listed below may give you an idea of those which would more or less suit you.

*A Scale*

```
P  |  |  |  |  |  |  |  |  |  |  |  |  |  |  |  |  |  |  |  |  A
   1  2  3  4  5  6  7  8  9  10 11 12 13 14 15 16 17 18 19 20
passive                                              aggressive
```

| | |
|---|---|
| bacteriologist | actor/actress |
| book-binder | bank manager |
| computer operator | beautician |
| dressmaker | broker |
| dietician | club manager |
| engraver | courier |
| gamekeeper | editor |
| gardener | entertainments officer |
| goldsmith | export salesperson |
| historian | fashion buyer |
| illustrator | hotel manager |
| library assistant | liberal studies teacher |
| lighthouse keeper | negotiator |
| patents examiner | publican |
| picture framer | public relations manager |
| potter | publisher |
| proof reader | reporter |
| storekeeper | speech and drama teacher |
| technical writer | transport manager |

## Should I work by myself?

People are important to you just as they are to everybody else. The often quoted statement 'No man is an island' is true. But some of us like to have more contact with people than others. There are various factors which determine whether we want to spend most of our time with people, and whether this should be with many people or just one or two. Some of us can only take people in small doses, feeling happier when we are working by ourselves, largely undisturbed. In some careers, the end product does not require much communication with others, for example if the work is highly specialised. But these are few and far between and some amount of social skill is present in almost every job. Whether you are going to be involved in management or as part of a work group or team, you will have to take some account of the necessity in most careers to associate with others.

## The characteristics of G

If you are high on the G scale you like to go along with people and feel that you belong. Wanting to be with people has nothing to do with aggression or self-confidence. In fact, a person who is very high on the G scale might well feel exposed on his own; he prefers to have others to turn to for assistance and advice. Such people often club together and are loyal to the team. They do not like to rock the boat, not because they are passive or sensitive but simply because they set a high value on team membership. At the other end of the scale is the independent-minded person who is inclined to make decisions alone rather than as part of a group. If you are low on the G scale you are not necessarily lacking in confidence but you prefer to be self-reliant. However, a low score often indicates some social shyness. Do you sometimes find it difficult to break the ice?

The advantage of being high on the G scale is that you are going to fit in extremely well. Your interest in people will literally cement a team together; you often bring out the best in people who will recognise and respond to this interest. Group loyalty and dependability are also useful characterisics, as is commitment to the team goals. You will do well in careers where interpersonal contact is necessary since you will relate to others quickly and easily.

On the negative side, the fact that you are a 'high G' personality implies some lack of individuality since you subordinate your own desires to some extent for the sake of the group. There may be some trade-off – such as originality for friendship. The very fact that you fit in can make you conventional and ordinary. Another issue which sometimes arises is that your fellow-feeling may prevent you from taking action which might offend others; the tendency to protect people you like may not be in the interests of the organisation. In fact, it may not even help the other person in the longer erm. For example, if you help to draw attention away from somebody who is not pulling his weight in an organisation you may not be doing the best thing to help your friend face up to the difficulty. This kind of behaviour indicates that for you, the business exists for the benefit of the people who work in it rather than for any other reason – such as making a product or even a profit!

## The characteristics of I

At the other end of the scale the indepent-minded person makes decisions alone. If you are low on G, this does not necessarily imply that you dislike people (though you might very well do so). You certainly feel that, when it comes to achieving what you want, you are going to do much better under your own steam. You probably do not like social situations very much. Projecting yourself in a group is something you simply have to endure.

Positive aspects of being independent-minded are the many opportunities open to you. A high value is still put on self-reliance in many jobs, where you may be in the company of others but can largely shut yourself off when it comes to doing your actual work. The important thing is for you not to have to depend on others for the way your work turns out, to be able to use your initiative in your own way. You may be able to see the direct results of your own efforts.

The big disadvantage of being independent-minded is that you can sometimes do things off your own bat of which others may not approve. People do not know what you are up to and you can lose touch as well. You may be given some highly specialised role which makes you something of an outsider. Although you might enjoy this, you can also lose out because you will not know what is going on in the mainstream of things. And of course, you won't mind very much if you don't get any Christmas cards, will you?

The above comments talk about extremes on the scale as do the remarks related to all the other scales. Mark your F score on the scale below and see which careers you tend to identify with.

## G Scale

I ┬┬┬┬┬┬┬┬┬┬┬┬┬┬┬┬┬┬┬┬ G
1 2 3 4 5 6 7 8 9 10 11 12 13 14 15 16 17 18 19 20

independent                                    group member

| | |
|---|---|
| accident assessor | air hostess/steward |
| archaeologist | auctioneer |
| architect | cashier |
| barrister | club manager |
| book-binder | club secretary |
| bus conductor | community worker |
| buyer | entertainments officer |
| chiropodist | fireman |
| courier | house parent |
| craftsperson | interviewer |
| dentist | masseur/masseuse |
| designer | play leader |
| engraver | publican |
| health visitor | public relations manager |
| interpreter | remedial teacher |
| literary agent | sailor |
| literary critic | salesperson |
| milkman | soldier |
| photographer | youth worker |
| printer | |
| proof reader | |
| publisher | |
| reporter | |
| shepherd | |
| silversmith | |
| train driver | |
| writer | |

# Looking at your total personality

Having examined your four individual traits in detail it is time to get the full picture. Transfer your individual scores to the FLAG graph on the next page, marking each appropriate place with an X as in the example.

*Example:*

Connect up your four scores. In the example, the results can be described as low, high, low, high (FLAG result: SLPG).

What should you do if your scores are in the middle or if some scores are relatively higher or lower? In these cases you must make your own judgement as to the tendency your FLAG test result shows. If your pattern is not absolutely clear, you may have to try out several of the combinations below which are close to your own results.

If you remain confused as to which FLAG description suits you best, you may have to do the test over again, trying to be more sharply aware of your personality as you do so. Alternatively, you may have a broad personality and be able to fit into many areas. For you, your aptitudes or your motivation are going to be more important in determining your career.

## FLAG test result

| | F | L | A | G | |
|---|---|---|---|---|---|
| High | 20 | 20 | 20 | 20 | High |
| | 18 | 18 | 18 | 18 | |
| | 16 | 16 | 16 | 16 | |
| | 14 | 14 | 14 | 14 | |
| | 12 | 12 | 12 | 12 | |
| | 10 | 10 | 10 | 10 | |
| | 8 | 8 | 8 | 8 | |
| | 6 | 6 | 6 | 6 | |
| | 4 | 4 | 4 | 4 | |
| | 2 | 2 | 2 | 2 | |
| Low | 0 | 0 | 0 | 0 | Low |
| | S | C | P | I | |

**My FLAG result is:** _____

## Typical personality combinations

The sixteen major combinations below can be used as a means
by which you can (a) understand yourself more clearly, and (b)
relate your own personality to broad types of work.

| | FLAG | Character |
|---|---|---|
| 1. | FLAG | Politician |
| 2. | FLAI | Entrepreneur |
| 3. | FLPG | Helper/Assistant |
| 4. | FCAG | Manager |
| 5. | SLAG | Campaigner |
| 6. | FLPI | Free agent |
| 7. | FCPG | Provider |
| 8. | SCAG | Teacher |
| 9. | SLAI | Artist |
| 10. | FCAI | Advocate |
| 11. | SLPG | Helping hand |
| 12. | FCPI | Specialist |

| 13. | SLPI | Rolling stone |
| 14. | SCAI | Adviser |
| 15. | SCPG | Supporter |
| 16. | SCPI | Loner |

## 1. The Politician (FLAG)

Your personality is predominantly factual, lively, aggressive and group-orientated. Although you may not have all these characteristics in the extreme, their presence is likely to help you in negotiating, campaigning and initiating activites which others need persuading to follow. You are likely to be active, engaged in many tasks and with many contacts. A feature of your personality is the ability to switch interests, moving quickly from one subject to the next. You are never lost for an answer for long. You are energetic and don't get beaten down so that you eventually get what you want. Although you have lots of projects, you seem to be able to fit new ones in. Others are happy to give you responsibility and look to you as leader because you have ideas, confidence, practicality and interpersonal skills.

You may be 'in politics' as a politician proper or in some associated role; numerous careers afford opportunities which are not obviously political in the traditional sense. You may be working in some part of government service but could also be in business, having particular interests in organisational structure and corporate development.

*Careers*

advertising executive
auctioneer
club secretary
estate agent
managing director

politician and political agent
public relations director
senior administrator
sports coach/manager

## 2. The Entrepreneur (FLAI)

Your personality is factual, lively, aggressive and independent. You show determination in getting what you want, maybe at the expense of others. There is no doubt about it – you show a lot of drive and strength of purpose. You will have a buoyant and energetic personality. You can spot opportunities and also apply yourself selectively to make those opportunities work for you. It is unlikely that you will allow yourself to be held back by petty considerations. You will often go your own way and back your own judgement against others more conservative than yourself.

Your enterprising and self-reliant style is frequently found in business and in other activities connected with wealth generation. It is the independent-mindedness which, among your other characteristics, is the key to your success because you are prepared to act on your initiative; you will do what you want and wait for others to catch up with you. Typically, you will pursue activites in which you can do things your own way and set your personal stamp on things. You will also expect to see a measurable statement of your success. There are innumerable careers open to you.

*Careers*

| | |
|---|---|
| agent (import/export) | property developer |
| buyer | publisher |
| marketing director | road manager |
| market trader | self-employed business person |

## 3. The Assistant (FLPG)

You are lively, passive and group-orientated. On the one hand you have a down-to-earth, stable quality which makes you solid and dependable. At the same time you are a conformist and fit in with others well. This combination allows you to come to the fore in situations requiring personal skills, particularly those of tact and understanding. Your own resourcefulness is much sought after by others who appreciate your comforting and reassuring manner. You are likely to be popular as well as admired; you will know what to do in a crisis, keeping your cool while all about you others are losing theirs. You will enjoy challenges but you like to apply the skills you have learned to overcome them. You find life interesting and enthusiasm rather than personal ambition is your main characteristic.

There are plenty of opportunities for you in all areas of work. In fact, your characteristics are so much in demand that you are unlikely to be out of a job. You fit well into the structure of many organisations and companies where your willingness and practicality are always appreciated.

*Careers*

| | |
|---|---|
| air hostess/steward | masseur/masseuse |
| bar person | play leader |
| dental assistant | receptionist |
| hairdresser | secretary |
| house parent | |

## . The Manager (FCAG)

You are factual, calm, aggressive and group-orientated. You are interested in people and have an excellent intuitive sense of what makes them tick. It will be of particular interest to you to be in charge of people in organisations where success can be judged by how well you achieve a task together. It is your aim to get things done with people and through people. Personally, you are organised and hard to ruffle. You enjoy planning ahead and marshalling your resources. You may distrust abstract or over-elaborate ideas, your own style being the product of experience and developed skills. You are likely to be methodical rather than inspiring, but at the same time, the fact that you don't take unmeasured risks means that you generally achieve what you want. Others feel confident in you and therefore you often find yourself in charge.

You will often 'keep things going' and make things work, particularly when people and materials are brought together. Ideally, you need to work in an organisation of some kind. You want either to deal with products or equipment or to work towards some real goal where you feel you could achieve something tangible.

*Careers*

| | |
|---|---|
| armed forces officer | general manager |
| bank manager | hotel manager |

| production manager | retail manager |
| publican | transport manager |

## 5. The Campaigner (SLAG)

You are sensitive, lively, aggressive and group-orientated These qualities mean that you are thoughtful towards people as well as full of ideas; you are aware and want to put things right. Your spontaneity and insight are admirable qualities Put these together with interpersonal flair and you have someone who take up causes. You are quick to spot injustice. All right, sometimes you may shoot your mouth off, but who cares – the point needed to be made! Your heart is in the right place, but you must be careful not to go off at a tangent. Your desire will be to do good, to make things better, to create a better world. You can be pushy and you may get emotionally involved: this is your strength, while your weakness is not knowing when to stop. However, people will often rely upon you to 'wield the cudgels' on their behalf.

You should look for careers in which people need a helping hand or someone to show them the way. You may supply the charisma and fortitude they lack. Be prepared for intense but short relationships at work as you move energetically and enthusiastically from project to project.

*Careers*

| beautician | public relations executive |
| civil rights worker | speech and drama teacher |
| courier | teacher |
| demonstrator | union representative |
| journalist | |

## 6. The Free Agent (FLPI)

You are factual, lively, passive and independent. You can therefore work in your own way and at your own pace. But you are also able to fit in with others, even being willing to adapt your own schedule to fit in with theirs. You are able to 'go along with things' and you don't let things get you down. You enjoy having a skill and you enjoy the certainty of

nowing what is expected of you. Relationships are on a basis
f mutual respect. You probably have a boss, but may work
nsupervised so that there is no one on your back.

You have the ability to apply your skills in new situations,
ut it is your skills and experience you rely upon as you are not
 great risk-taker. Your self-reliance and liveliness are fre-
uently misinterpreted as management potential. This may
ppeal to you at times, but it is not really what you want
ecause it alters your relationships with people; you suddenly
nd yourself worrying about people and you prefer to be a free
gent. Another thing to watch for is that you do not rely
oo much on a trade or skills which will become outmoded.
ven so, you are very adaptable and hence very retrainable.

*Careers*

| | |
|---|---|
| ccounting technician | office machinery mechanic |
| us conductor | painter and decorator |
| hef/cook | paramedic |
| himney sweep | repairer |
| ietician | road patrol officer |
| nterpreter | surgeon |

## . The Provider (FCPG)

ou are factual, calm, passive and group-orientated. While
vanting to be with people, you have no desire to take charge;
ou want to fit in and usually do. You are not the type to ruffle
thers' feathers but will go along with the wishes of the
najority. The stability and reassurance you present to the
vorld make you accepted as a friend and as a trustworthy
ssistant. You do not get side-tracked by the irrelevant nor do
ou take on projects which are too large. In fact, you are
easonable in all things. You feel most comfortable where
here is order and planning. Change is not your style – unless,
hat is, all the risks have been taken out.

You act as a constant, reliable force in keeping people
ogether and your predictability and dependability make you a
;reat team member. You are a mine of useful experience and
nformation which others can rely upon. Preferred careers are

likely to be in factual concerns, such as doing or making something practical. You will probably be actively involved in a team effort.

*Careers*

| | |
|---|---|
| agricultural secretary | merchant seaman |
| ambulance crew | nurse |
| Armed Forces member | police officer |
| cashier | prison officer |
| fireman | road gang worker |
| guard | |

## 8. The Teacher (SCAG)

You are sensitive, calm, aggressive and group-orientated. This combination of traits allows you to deal with an often demanding and hectic environment. But would you have it any other way? You are likely to be in tune with what is going on. In particular, you will pick up nuances in the behaviour of others. You will be quick to see ideas and possibilities. But you will also be consistent and firm. You will mix with others easily – and not just at work either, since you enjoy being responsible for others in your spare time as well. You will see another's point of view but you are also determined and have plenty of ideas of your own.

It is likely that you will have a definite skill or experience to offer. In fact, you are probably something of an expert. But it is unlikely to be the subject or content of your work which appeals to you so much as the opportunity to pass your knowledge and skill on to others. In many ways you are a leader, but due to your strong altruism and sensitivity you are rather more attracted to public service than diplomacy or business.

*Careers*

| | |
|---|---|
| doctor | senior teacher |
| osteopath | social worker |
| psychologist | training officer |
| senior nursing officer | youth worker |

## 9. The Artist (SLAI)

You are sensitive, lively, aggressive and independent. Ideas and expression are essential to you. You are often described as radical or impractical. In your search for novelty you can become uncomfortable and apparently at odds with the world. You are thoughtful and reflective, but have a sharp mind which quickly recognises dissonance in many spheres. The need to survive can make you tough. At times you can have a defensive or prickly quality, owing to the strength of your feelings and principles. You can feel impassioned by both emotional and abstract matters. Thus, you vent your feelings in your art while you may harangue others about politics and the state of the world. It is unlikely that you mix much though relationships are probably intense, even stormy. With you, both socially and personally, it is all or nothing.

You need to work largely by yourself as you soon feel bored in a group; you have some unique idea and you need to work on it in your own way. Communication with others is most successful when you can present to them – in other words, when you make a 'statement'. What you create may be larger than life or it may be a distillation. The ordinary everyday world is unsatisfactory; you will take it and abstract the epitome and quintessential. As you can be both entertaining and challenging you will find opportunities in activities which others find diverting and thought-provoking.

*Careers*

| | |
|---|---|
| architect | interior designer |
| artist | musician |
| author | sculptor |
| dancer | |

## 10. The Advocate (FCAI)

You are factual, calm, aggressive and independent. These qualities make you formidable. The facts are at your disposal, you are clear about them and you can present them calmly and logically. There is no question of intuition. You will keep ideas and information to yourself. You will find yourself happiest in debate or at least in the presence of similarly sharp minds uncorrupted by sentimentality or lack of training. In fact, you set a lot of store by your own mind which you have, with some pride, honed to a sharp point. Essentially, you are self-reliant. People need you to sort out their problems, but relationships will be businesslike as opposed to friendly. It is the business or the point at issue that brings you together with others, rather than fellow-feeling.

You will do well in careers in which you need to keep your head, such as those situations where others get flustered, forget what they are saying, don't stick to the facts and take too much on trust. Your investigative and detached style is suited to careers where the objective truth needs to be ascertained and where there are legal or measurable issues to deal with.

*Careers*

| | |
|---|---|
| barrister | police inspector |
| customs officer | solicitor |
| dentist | work study officer |

## 11. The Helping Hand (SLPG)

You are sensitive, lively, passive and group-oriented. Others will find you interesting, responsive and want to be with you. Your main attribute is your willingness to try new things. You are eager and expressive. Lively situations appeal to you and you are happy when there's plenty going on; you are bored by routine and predictable situations. You probably hate figures and office work has very little appeal. As you are intuitive and creative you need an artistic environment, but you may lack the assertiveness and be too well-disposed towards people to be a really successful artist in your own right. Second, then, is your need to associate with a team, to feel yourself part of a project. A group undertaking, where your own skills and personality complement those of others, will suit you best. You will never lack friends as you are such good fun to be with; your enthusiasm for life is infectious. At the same time, you may never settle at anything for very long because you tend to exchange stability for new opportunities.

Careers in which you find novelty as well as a group to identify with will suit you. You like to achieve quickly, so careers which require lots of study or preparation will not be so attractive.

*Careers*

| | |
|---|---|
| chef/cook | receptionist |
| dresser | retail assistant |
| marketing assistant | stage-hand |
| nursery nurse | waiter/waitress |

## 12. The Specialist (FCPI)

You are factual, calm, passive and independent. In other words, you have a clear, sharp and detached mind, uncluttered by the trivial or irrelevant. You are capable of applying yourself well to resolving problems. You are technically minded because you see issues logically. Typically, you work deductively: you are a glutton for knowledge and see the connections between apparently diverse bits of information. You fit in with people easily enough but will not socialise much because you 'have things to do'. Your life is well ordered and there are lots of things you want to get on with. You are frequently described as efficient. Others call upon you to help them solve problems, though not those of an intuitive nature. You appear to lack some of the human faults that so beset others and your 'pick yourself up and get on with it' attitude can be unnerving to those with less energy and self-reliance. Your usefulness arises from your organised approach and your expert background; your advice will be valuable because it is objective. However, it would be a mistake to believe that your technique and expertise could enable you to be a leader, because this requires a social sensibility which is not one of your strong points.

*Careers*

| | |
|---|---|
| accounting technician | diver |
| actuary | driver |
| archivist | engineer |
| auditor | operational researcher |

| | |
|---|---|
| patents examiner | systems analyst |
| rating valuation officer | technician |
| referee | train driver |
| scientist | |

## 13. The Rolling Stone (SLPI)

You are sensitive, lively, passive and independent. If anything is important to you, it is not to get over-involved. Long and close contacts with people are particularly to be avoided. People should preferably stay at a distance: you do not make demands upon others and you would prefer it if they did not make demands upon you. Many things interest you but you will pursue few to a conclusion. You have a restless disposition that is hard to satisfy in the long term; you are not studious and tend to move on. On the other hand, you may have a wealth of scattered knowledge. The problem is to find a means of bringing it all together and applying it in some useful way. Unless you are careful, you may find yourself forever on the edge of things, flirting with people and with different activities. You are good fun in a social setting and when matters are light rather than serious you can be entertaining and even original.

What you achieve in your career may be determined largely by your early education; as you are not disciplined yourself, your early schooling may have led to success (and therefore entry qualifications) which you would not have obtained under your own steam. Generally, the work you do will depend upon luck and opportunity rather than your own fixed purpose in shaping your own destiny.

*Careers*

| | |
|---|---|
| bar person | porter |
| dancer | production worker |
| disc jockey | shop assistant |
| entertainer | waiter/waitress |
| model | |

## 14. The Adviser (SCAI)

You are sensitive, calm, aggressive and independent. People as well as ideas fascinate you, but you may stay detached rather than becoming personally involved. You find the arts more appealing than technical subjects, but your steadiness makes you less of an artist than a commentator or critic. Again, the detached or logical element of your personality may lead to your shaping some world view of your own; you may have a philosophical bent. But rather than comment you like to get out and do – in other words, you like to test your theories in action. Although you work with people and may have an influential role, you remain essentially an outsider rather than insider. Nevertheless, you can establish contact easily and you have qualifications and experience as well as an authoritative manner.

You can sell your skills as some kind of consultant (though this may not be the actual title of your job). Part of your talent is your timing – knowing that others are ready to receive your initiatives. One drawback is that you can be too theoretical at times and this affects your relationships as well as the work itself. However, you are good value in 'pointing the way to go', in indicating how things ought to be in an ideal world.

*Careers*

analyst
business adviser/consultant
human resources consultant
journalist

librarian
social scientist
training officer

## 15. The Supporter (SCPG)

You are sensitive, calm, passive and group-oriented. You probably allow others to make the running. Indeed, it seems that you put yourself out for others. You certainly have insight and you have probably acquired useful skills which enable you to contribute very effectively to the well-being of others. Not only are you thoughtful and aware but you apply yourself consistently and calmly to making the most of your talents. You are a valuable addition to any team. You fit in easily and no one feels threatened by you. In fact, people like you a lot because they recognise that you like them and are prepared to care for them. They will unload their troubles on you and receive sympathy as well as skilled advice in return. You work well in a team where your skills complement those of others or where everybody's skills are the same. In this respect, you are essentially democratic and sharing. You enjoy being appreciated and valued and you resent being used or exploited. You have a strong inner motivation which makes you resist and back away if given orders.

You will find yourself in a career which demands insight, application and interpersonal skills. You are in many ways similar to the Helper but your skills are more on the human side rather than providing technical help.

*Careers*

| | |
|---|---|
| counsellor | nursery teacher |
| hospital porter | remedial teacher |
| house parent | social worker |
| mental nurse | therapist |

## 16. The Loner (SCPI)

You are sensitive, calm, passive and independent. You want to work by yourself and are capable of doing so. It is not so much that you will forge ahead or leave others behind but a question of wanting to find a niche for yourself. Because you do not need much contact with people, you might read a lot or have other interests to occupy you. Characterised by intelligence, thoughtfulness and possibly even a gruff courtesy, you prefer to be detached. Shyness is a feature which may be misinterpreted as grumpiness or hostility: it is just your defensiveness and desire to remain in your own world. You are interested in many things, thoughtful and aware, but far-sighted rather than near-sighted. Although difficult to get to know, you can be intensely loyal. You have definite opinions and are slow to change.

Choose a career in which you can apply yourself in your own way and at your own pace. Although you may have plenty of contact with people, it is likely to be an incidental rather than a major feature of your work. Plenty of jobs give you the isolation and freedom you like. In most of them you will be working for an employer, unless you have an artistic skill which you can sell.

*Careers*

| | |
|---|---|
| arborist | lighthouse keeper |
| curator | milkman |
| dressmaker | potter |
| farmworker | shepherd |
| gardener | thatcher |
| historian | |

## Chapter 4

# Movitation: What Do I Want to Do?

In some ways, motivation is even more important than ability or personality. You can probably think of examples of your own to support this view. How many people have you known with ability who have apparently just not bothered about achievement? Alternatively, you may also know and have certainly heard of people who have triumphed over all odds, who have 'made it' in something which they seemed completely unsuited for, who overcame disasters to win fame and fortune. What makes some of us go on when others give up? What makes some of us break out from our humble origins while others are trapped by their background? What is and is not possible for most of us is very largely determined by motivation.

The strength of the motivational factor is nowhere better exemplified than in the contrast between success in the 'real world' and educational/exam prowess. It is a strange fact that the educational system, with its selective approach to establishing academic excellence, is a poor predictor of success in later life. Thus, the School Dunce drops out at the earliest opportunity and becomes an Errand Boy, then a Trader, then a Merchant and finally a Businessman. He might employ business graduates and professional people to make even more money for him. Again, some intellectually able people fail to make the most of their potential because they lack the energy, drive, or direction – all synonyms for motivation.

We can be motivated by many things: fear, love, envy, compassion. At a fundamental level, motivation arises from fears attached to deep and basic survival needs originating in our animal ancestry. Starvation is a powerful motivator! But once basic needs are satisfied, we begin to be motivated by activities which we enjoy for their own sake, not because they are necessary for our essential existence.

In most people's minds, a career comes mid-way between survival and enjoyment. Nowadays, it is not necessary for most of us to actually work in order to survive. Nobody is likely to starve to death. But if you want anything more than the basic essentials to keep you fed and sheltered then work will be important.

Is any kind of work going to be satisfactory and continually motivating? Are you prepared to trade your time and labour for a wage? Many people think in this way. What they are saying is in effect, 'I put up with my job because it provides me with the money to enjoy my leisure time.' This is an 'economic' view of work because it represents the exchange of labour for cash. It leads to the 'carrot and stick' principle of employment. As a philosophy it is far less popular with employees as well as employers than in the past. In an age where welfare benefits take the edge off the fear of destitution and extend in many cases to the provision of what 50 years ago would be called 'luxury' items, the idea of enjoyment at work as a motivator has arisen. It has become clear to employers that employees who enjoy doing their work are more productive than those who do not. It is no longer a case of wanting to work out of fear but wanting to work out of the satisfaction that the activity itself provides.

Your work will bring you various kinds of reward, but some of these will be intangible, such as contentment, satisfaction, respect, importance and affection. Fortunately, we are not all motivated by the same things and the opportunities open to us are diverse and innumerable.

At this stage in the book it will be clear to you that each of us is born with a unique intellectual structure and a unique personality structure, and of course we grow up in a unique situation. The influences upon us, particularly during childhood, prod and poke us in different directions. All the time we are testing out our hereditary potential against our environment. Sometimes we win, sometimes we lose (where winning can be defined as achieving that which makes us happy and losing as experiencing that which we find painful).

It is not always as clear cut as this since few of us are ever really free agents. In other words, not all of us have the same opportunities and many of us therefore feel blocked or curbed, never having been really able to try out all our talents or express ourselves fully. Maybe we encountered disapproval from adults. Maybe the courses we had to take at school never really suited us; we merely went along with what our parents expected. If we had known ourselves fully and known how to express ourselves in order to get what we wanted we would have gone in a different direction.

Nevertheless, most people have a pretty good chance as they grow up of finding out just what motivates them and what does not. What classes at school did you go to willingly or less willingly? What do you prefer to watch on TV? What do you do in your spare time? Is it maths or cookery? Do you prefer sport or reading? Do you like to go out with friends or watch television? In various ways, your motivation will have been 'shaped up'. There is a rich source of information all around you and you will have explored lots of possibilities, either directly as a participant or vicariously as an observer. You will have been mentally processing this information: picking it up, weighing, discarding, trying out, keeping or throwing it away.

Some things you like the sound of may not be immediately available but perhaps you are sufficiently motivated to get nearer to what you want. You may have to study in order to get even closer to the kind of activity which appeals to you. And all the time, through meeting people, reading, watching TV etc you are making connections about how different careers interlock with certain kinds of aptitudes and personalities, and the different kinds of reward they provide. Consciously or subconsciously you will continually match yourself against the various possibilities. As you discover patterns in your own motivation and get to know yourself better, you will imprint this self-knowledge figuratively speaking upon the multitude of opportunities which present themselves. You will become aware that some of these patterns match better than others.

So how is it that with all this rich experience you still remain uncertain about what really motivates you? It may be that your interests have developed only on the basis of what has been available to you. Possibly you have already succeeded in something you were good at but feel you have other ideas to explore. Again, perhaps you have heard about lots of careers but find it difficult to know what they really involve. For example, you were a good swimmer at school but does this mean that you will enjoy being a diver?; you were good at maths but what does becoming an economist entail?; you started in the family business but never really felt fulfilled so would it be a good idea to return to study and, if so, what?

It could also be that your motivation has changed. Although this rarely happens quickly, it can do so over the years.

Finally, it is because many of us are motivated by a number of things which often seem in conflict with each other that we need to look carefully at the strength and direction of our motivation.

The motivation questionnaire allows you to look at your own personal motivation in a structured and practical way. It is designed to bring you down to earth. Stop dreaming, sort yourself out, get on and do it!

## The motivation questionnaire

This is designed to investigate one important aspect of your motivation – that which is directed towards a career. The way the questionnaire works is to help you to make decisions about which among your interests is more or less important to you.

Although you may feel that you could develop new interests if you understood what was involved, your experience so far must be the starting point. However, the questionnaire often provides some surprising results. Perhaps because it can reveal and highlight possibilities in a systematic and meaningful way it can often bring into focus those areas of work which you perceive as giving you the most opportunity to express yourself – not only to obtain reward but also to find enjoyment and personal satisfaction in ways that only you can define.

The questionnaire is in two parts: it asks first what jobs and second what activities appeal to you. It is important for you to have some idea of the 'frame of mind' you are in as you take the questionnaire. Let us be clear about what this means. You could find yourself eliminating some of the alternatives because (a) you do not have the qualifications to do the job or (b) you do not think you could get the qualifications to do the job. Do not concern yourself with these issues; find out what appeals to you first, then let the ability tests assess whether you could do the job or not. In other words, if you do the questionnaire in a 'narrow' frame of mind, you might cut yourself off from some of the possibilities before you even start, because you will in effect be saying to yourself 'Oh, I couldn't do that (even though I might like to.)'

Another frame of mind to avoid at this stage is one which is over-concerned with (c) pay or (d) status. There are many such considerations which could have a bearing upon your decision and it would be impossile to weigh them all in the balance; the best thing is to ignore them as far as you can. Simply ask yourself whether the occupation or activity appeals to you *in a general way*. It is the impression it makes on you which counts – you can evaluate your underlying reasons and the various circumstances which led you to make specific choices later. Remember, your results in the ability and personality tests will give you more concrete evidence of your suitability for a particular area of work than will your own opinion.

If you feel that it is impossible to divest your mind entirely of certain realistic and practical considerations, the best thing to do is to take the motivation questionnaire twice, putting yourself each time into a different frame of mind. You can then see how the results compare. For example, you might complete it 'realistically' the first time and the second time just 'let yourself go'.

Some of the choices you are forced to make in this questionnaire you will find will be easy; others will be difficult because both occupations will appear either equally dull or equally appealing. However, the questionnaire uses a 'forced choice' technique, which establishes a picture of the relative attractiveness of certain kinds of activity.

People sometimes object to choosing between two things they like equally or dislike equally. The forced choice compels ou to make a decision. When we see that you do, on balance, prefer some types of activity to others, this information can be used to point to the specific careers that accord with your preferred interests.

There is no time limit to this questionnaire though you should not spend too long making choices. First impressions are generally as useful as decisions arrived at after much deliberation. Whether you work quickly or slowly through the questionnaire will not affect the result significantly.

Try to do each part of the motivation questionnaire without interruption. There is no reason why you should not have a break of whatever length you like between Parts 1 and 2. Both parts of the questionnaire are to be completed in the same way: you look at two occupations or two descriptions of an occupational activity and decide which one appeals to you more. It is a good idea to look up those careers which you do not know much about in order to see what they involve.

When choosing between the two careers or descriptions you have three points to award. If one occupation or description appeals to you more than the alternative you can give it three points and the other no points. If you are not sure, give the job you marginally prefer two points and the alternative one point. Give more points to the career or the description which has more appeal. You must always give away three points, no more, no less.

The points you have awarded should be written in the circles opposite the occupational titles or descriptions. In the first example, which has been done for you below, it is quite clear what sort of activity has the greater appeal.

Interpreter ③

Gardener ⓪

In the next example, the person has had more difficulty in deciding upon which activity he would rather undertake. On balance, he has decided to divide the points.

Manager of cinema ①

Work with formulae and equations ②

Take no notice of the letters at the head of each column for the moment (the purpose of these will be explained later).

Now you are ready to take the motivation questionnaire.

# The motivation questionnaire

## Part 1

|  | | L | C | S | X | R | P | A |
|---|---|---|---|---|---|---|---|---|
| 1. | (a) Publicity agent | | | | 0 | | | |
|  | (b) Writer | | | 3 | | | | |
| 2. | (a) Geologist | | | | | 3 | | |
|  | (b) Nurse | | | 0 | | | | |
| 3. | (a) Financial analyst | | | | | | | 0 |
|  | (b) Play leader | | | 3 | | | | |
| 4. | (a) Astronomer | | | | | 3 | | |
|  | (b) Gunsmith | | | | | 0 | | |
| 5. | (a) Auditor | | | | | | | 0 |
|  | (b) Silversmith | | | | | 3 | | |
| 6. | (a) Quantity surveyor | | | | | | | 0 |
|  | (b) Poet | | 3 | | | | | |
| 7. | (a) Probation officer | | | 0 | | | | |
|  | (b) Oceanographer | | | | | 3 | | |
| 8. | (a) Personnel manager | | | 0 | | | | |
|  | (b) Programmer | | | | | | | 3 |
| 9. | (a) Accident assessor | | | | | | | 0 |
|  | (b) Composer for a rock band | | 3 | | | | | |
| 10. | (a) Tractor driver | | | | | | 0 | |
|  | (b) Auctioneer | | | 0 | | | | |

**119**

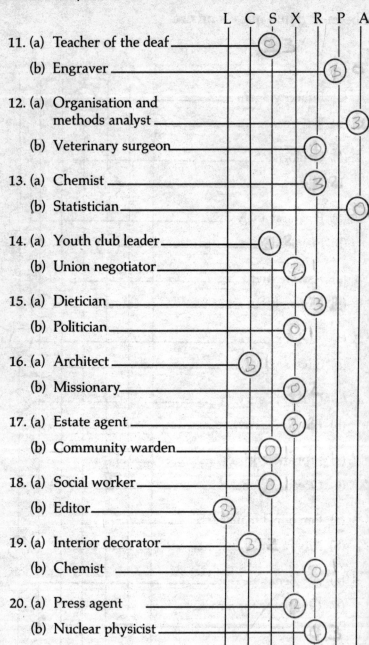

|  | | L | C | S | X | R | P | A |
|---|---|---|---|---|---|---|---|---|
| 11. | (a) Teacher of the deaf | | | 0 | | | | |
| | (b) Engraver | | | | | | 3 | |
| 12. | (a) Organisation and methods analyst | | | | | | | 3 |
| | (b) Veterinary surgeon | | | | 0 | | | |
| 13. | (a) Chemist | | | | 3 | | | |
| | (b) Statistician | | | | | | | 0 |
| 14. | (a) Youth club leader | | 1 | | | | | |
| | (b) Union negotiator | | 2 | | | | | |
| 15. | (a) Dietician | | | | | 3 | | |
| | (b) Politician | | | | 0 | | | |
| 16. | (a) Architect | | 3 | | | | | |
| | (b) Missionary | | | | 0 | | | |
| 17. | (a) Estate agent | | | | 3 | | | |
| | (b) Community warden | | | 0 | | | | |
| 18. | (a) Social worker | | | 0 | | | | |
| | (b) Editor | L | 3 | | | | | |
| 19. | (a) Interior decorator | | 3 | | | | | |
| | (b) Chemist | | | | | 0 | | |
| 20. | (a) Press agent | | 2 | | | | | |
| | (b) Nuclear physicist | | | | | 1 | | |

| | | L | C | S | X | R | P | A |
|---|---|---|---|---|---|---|---|---|
| 1. | (a) Journalist | 3 | | | | | | |
| | (b) Teacher | | | 0 | | | | |
| 22. | (a) Accountant | | | | | | | 0 |
| | (b) Public relations executive | | | | 3 | | | |
| 23. | (a) Car salesman | | | | 1 | | | |
| | (b) Upholsterer | | | | | | 2 | |
| 24. | (a) Photographer | | 3 | | | | | |
| | (b) Tax inspector | | | | | | | 0 |
| 25. | (a) Librarian | | 3 | | | | | |
| | (b) Bookkeeper | | | | | | | 0 |
| 26. | (a) Radio announcer | | | | 3 | | | |
| | (b) Economist | | | | | | | 0 |
| 27. | (a) Novelist | | 3 | | | | | |
| | (b) Horticulturalist | | | | | | 0 | |
| 28. | (a) Physical training instructor | | | 0 | | | | |
| | (b) Fashion designer | | 3 | | | | | |
| 29. | (a) Playwright | | 3 | | | | | |
| | (b) Experimental psychologist | | | | | 0 | | |
| 30. | (a) Forester | | | | | | 0 | |
| | (b) Metalurgist | | | | 3 | | | |

121

|  | L | C | S | X | R | P | A |
|---|---|---|---|---|---|---|---|
| 31. (a) Toymaker | | | | | | 3 | |
| (b) Window dresser | | 0 | | | | | |
| 32. (a) Graphic designer | | 3 | | | | | |
| (b) Medical social worker | | | 0 | | | | |
| 33. (a) Mechanical engineer | | | | | 0 | | |
| (b) Book critic | 3 | | | | | | |
| 34. (a) Bacteriologist | | | | | 0 | | |
| (b) Musician | | | 3 | | | | |
| 35. (a) Author | 3 | | | | | | |
| (b) Stage designer | | 0 | | | | | |
| 36. (a) Illustrator | | 3 | | | | | |
| (b) Demonstrator | | | | 0 | | | |
| 37. (a) Instrument maker | | | | | 3 | | |
| (b) Bank official | | | | | | | 0 |
| 38. (a) Composer | | 3 | | | | | |
| (b) Advertising copy-writer | 0 | | | | | | |
| 39. (a) Forensic scientist | | | | 0 | | | |
| (b) Actor | | 3 | | | | | |
| 40. (a) Electronics technician | | | | | 3 | | |
| (b) Art dealer | | 0 | | | | | |
| 41. (a) Solicitor | | 3 | | | | | |
| (b) Sales executive | | | | 0 | | | |

|  | | L | C | S | X | R | P | A |
|---|---|---|---|---|---|---|---|---|
| 2. (s) | Chef | | | | | | 3 | |
| (b) | Careers officer | | 0 | | | | | |

| Part 1 Totals | 33 | 27 | 4 | 17 | 19 | 20 | 6 |
|---|---|---|---|---|---|---|---|

*(not to be completed until Part 2 of the motivation questionnaire has been done)*

## Part 2

|  | | L | C | S | X | R | P | A |
|---|---|---|---|---|---|---|---|---|
| 1. (a) | Make a set of clay coffee pots and mugs | | | | | | 3 | |
| (b) | Establish a stock control system | | | | | | | 0 |
| 2. (a) | Learn how to screen print | | | 3 | | | | |
| (b) | Upholster an old sofa | | | | | | 0 | |
| 3. (a) | Look through a microscope and record findings | | | | | 3 | | |
| (b) | Learn how to audit and prepare a balance sheet | | | | | | | 0 |
| 4. (a) | Give English lessons to foreigners | 0 | | | | | | |
| (b) | Manage a pop group | | | | 3 | | | |
| 5. (a) | Learn how to repair a car | | | | | | 3 | |
| (b) | Run a household budget system | | | | | | | 0 |

| | L | C | S | X | R | P | A |
|---|---|---|---|---|---|---|---|
| 6. (a) Analyse plants to find new drugs | | | | | 3 | | |
| (b) Shape a piece of wood on a lathe | | | | | | 0 | |
| 7. (a) Nurse elderly people | | | 0 | | | | |
| (b) Design wallpaper | | | 3 | | | | |
| 8. (a) Interview job applicants | | 2 | | | | | |
| (b) Weave cloth | | | | | | 0 | |
| 9. (a) Design advertising posters | | 0 | | | | | |
| (b) Look out for suitable scripts to be published | 3 | | | | | | |
| 10. (a) Rewrite old books in modern English | 0 | 2 | | | | | |
| (b) Construct scale models | | | | | 3 | | |
| 11. (a) Learn a computer language | | | | | | | 3 |
| (b) Run courses for sales personnel | | | | 0 | 2 | | |
| 12. (a) Take a course in art appreciation | | 1 | | | | | |
| (b) Make a mould for figures and objects | | | | | | 2 | |
| 13. (a) Work out population statistics with a calculator | | | | | | | 0 |
| (b) Paint a stage set | | 3 | | | | | |

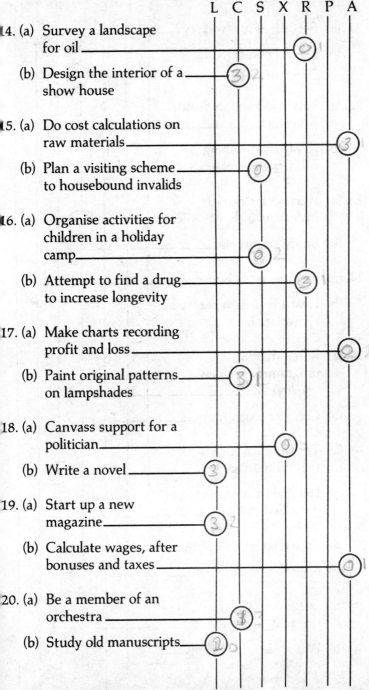

L C S X R P A

14. (a) Survey a landscape for oil — R: 0

(b) Design the interior of a show house — C: 3

15. (a) Do cost calculations on raw materials — A: 3

(b) Plan a visiting scheme to housebound invalids — S: 0

16. (a) Organise activities for children in a holiday camp — S: 0

(b) Attempt to find a drug to increase longevity — R: 3

17. (a) Make charts recording profit and loss — A: 0

(b) Paint original patterns on lampshades — C: 3

18. (a) Canvass support for a politician — R: 0

(b) Write a novel — C: 3

19. (a) Start up a new magazine — C: 3

(b) Calculate wages, after bonuses and taxes — A: 0

20. (a) Be a member of an orchestra — C: 3

(b) Study old manuscripts — C: 2

|  | | L | C | S | X | R | P | A |
|---|---|---|---|---|---|---|---|---|
| 21. | (a) Set stones in jewellery | | | | | | 3 | |
| | (b) Co-ordinate a local action group | | | | 0 | | | |
| 22. | (a) Give a lecture on health education | | | 0 | | | | |
| | (b) Apply the finishing touches to an object | | | | | | 3 | |
| 23. | (a) Auction articles left over from a charity sale | | | | 2 | | | |
| | (b) Study sea urchins | | | | | 1 | | |
| 24. | (a) Rewire an old house | | | | | | 2 | |
| | (b) Give a course in poetry appreciation | 0 | | | | | | |
| 25. | (a) Run a training programme for new employees | | | | 3 | | | |
| | (b) Conduct coach tours | | | 0 | | | | |
| 26. | (a) Try to find a cure for the common cold | | | | | 3 | | |
| | (b) Help run a centre for disturbed children | | | 0 | | | | |
| 27. | (a) Take wedding portraits | | 3 | | | | | |
| | (b) Negotiate with unions | | | | 0 | | | |
| 28. | (a) Design new scientific research equipment | | | | | 0 | | |
| | (b) Write television scripts | | 3 | | | | | |

L C S X R P A

29. (a) Discover artificial fibres — ③ (under R)

(b) Speak at a political rally — ⓪ (under X)

30. (a) Write a guide to TV programmes for a newspaper — ③ (under S)

(b) Discover new sources of food — ⓪ (under R)

31. (a) Write freelance articles — ③ (under L)

(b) Listen to people's problems — ⓪ (under X)

32. (a) Chair a committee — ⓪ (under X)

(b) Construct a rock garden and pool — ③ (under P)

33. (a) Counsel married couples — ③ (under S)

(b) Prepare financial reports for directors' meetings — ⓪ (under A)

34. (a) Prepare a play with a drama group — ③ (under S)

(b) Help people who have reading problems — ⓪ (under S)

35. (a) Give advice to people on how to pay less tax — ⓪ (under A)

(b) Write slogans for advertisements — ③ (under C)

36. (a) Repair broken objects or equipment — ③ (under P)

**127**

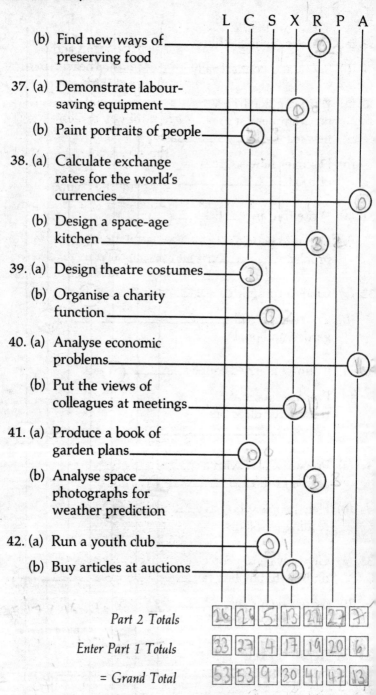

|  | L | C | S | X | R | P | A |
|---|---|---|---|---|---|---|---|
| (b) Find new ways of preserving food | | | | | 0 | | |
| 37. (a) Demonstrate labour-saving equipment | | | | 0 | | | |
| (b) Paint portraits of people | | 3 | | | | | |
| 38. (a) Calculate exchange rates for the world's currencies | | | | | | | 0 |
| (b) Design a space-age kitchen | | | | | 3 | | |
| 39. (a) Design theatre costumes | | 3 | | | | | |
| (b) Organise a charity function | | | 0 | | | | |
| 40. (a) Analyse economic problems | | | | | | | 1 |
| (b) Put the views of colleagues at meetings | | | | 2 | | | |
| 41. (a) Produce a book of garden plans | | 0 | | | | | |
| (b) Analyse space photographs for weather prediction | | | | | 3 | | |
| 42. (a) Run a youth club | | | 0 | | | | |
| (b) Buy articles at auctions | | | | 3 | | | |

| | L | C | S | X | R | P | A |
|---|---|---|---|---|---|---|---|
| *Part 2 Totals* | 16 | 26 | 5 | 13 | 24 | 27 | 7 |
| *Enter Part 1 Totals* | 33 | 27 | 4 | 17 | 19 | 20 | 6 |
| *= Grand Total* | 53 | 53 | 9 | 30 | 41 | 47 | 13 |

# The motivation graph

Turn first to the answers you gave in Part 1 and add up the figures in each column. Start with the column headed by the letter L. Count the total and put the figure at the bottom of the page. Do the same with the C, S, X, R, P and A columns. Continue in this way for each page until you can enter your total for Part 1 in the box provided. If you have done this correctly the combined scores of the seven columns should come to 126.

Do exactly the same with Part 2. Again, the column totals should equal 126. Now add the totals for the two parts together to get a grand total.

You can mark your score on the motivation graph on the next page. You will now see what the capital letters stand for. Draw a line across the point where your score falls. Do this with all seven scores. Then shade upwards from the bottom of the graph to this point. You will then have a profile of your motivation. It may look something like the graph below.

## Your motivation graph

| | Literary L | Creative C | Social S | Executive X | Research R | Practical P | Administrative A |
|---|---|---|---|---|---|---|---|

## Interpreting your motivational results

Do your graphical results make sense to you? They should provide you with a system of preferences, a hierarchy which ranges from the strongest area of attraction to the weakest. The simplest way to proceed from here is to suggest that you pursue your areas of high motivation and avoid your low ones.

Look at both your high and your low scores. What is high or low will depend upon your own profile, but most people get some scores which are in the 'above average' range as well as some which are in the 'below average' range. If some of your scores are 'average', this indicates that you do not currently have particularly strong feelings one way or the other about this sphere of activity.

For most people a score higher than 48 suggests strong

motivation and of course the higher the score, the stronger the preference for that occupational area. Conversely, scores below 24 will usually indicate areas which have very little appeal to you. Unless you feel you'd like to know more about what is actually involved in terms of work, you should probably avoid them.

You may have been asking yourself why there were two parts to the motivation questionnaire. The aim was to get as broad a picture as possible of you. The first part was based on the career titles which might appeal to you and the second dealt with career activities associated with them. The closer the scores you gained in Parts 1 and 2, the clearer your conception of your motivation will be. If there is a wide discrepancy between the two scores in any area of motivation, this would suggest that your knowledge of careers in the area concerned is not very high. A difference of more than about ten points does not matter but a wider discrepancy may indicate that your motivation will change once you know more about the careers which fall into this category.

If there are no great differences in your scores – that is, no sharply defined extremes – this means either (a) you do not know very much about yourself, (b) you do not know what is involved in different areas of work, (c) you may be multi-talented but helpless in the face of so many opportunities, or (d) nothing much appeals to you at all! In all these instances, the ability and personality tests will be of greater value in defining what would motivate you if you were more aware of your potential.

What happens if your motivation results appear to be saying that you do not like the career you are in, eg if you are a business executive and your results seem to indicate that you want to be an artist? Do you give everything up and move to the Left Bank in Paris? Not at all. The questionnaire is subtle and the answers it gives are sometimes directional rather than specific. In this case, it is not necessarily saying that your present job is wrong for you, merely that you would like more opportunity to do things your own way, to be creative. Perhaps you can achieve this in your present work, with a little reorientation. Or perhaps you really should give it all up and move to the *Rive Gauche*. In the end, you are the best person to evaluate the real meaning of your results: you are the one who has to make the decisions.

Some people obtain one strong area of motivation which makes interpretation comparatively simple. Others get two or even three peaks of motivation so that having to combine these in a career becomes much more difficult. In fact, if there are three areas it may be useful to consult a careers counsellor to help you make sense of your results (though you should be able to put the elements together more or less by yourself). Take time to think through your results and ask yourself, 'What could I do which is basically concerned with . . ., but which has a little of . . . and where I am occasionally involved with . . .?' You may find yourself becoming quite inventive. And truth to say, there are many jobs which contain numerous elements, so it is by no means impossible to find a job which contains all the pieces you require to motivate you fully.

The following pages contain broad areas of career motivation, together with lists of careers which fit roughly into them. Within each area there are careers of great diversity. For example, in the Practical area you will find both lock keeper and locksmith. The former is involved in outdoor work which often requires heavy physical movement; the latter works mainly indoors and the mechanical movements are frequently intricate. Look at the seven major areas of motivation and you can then break each career down further to see which part of it would or would not appeal. In doing so, you might find that the Practical area appeals to you most, but you might reject an individual career because it is perhaps too administrative or not sufficiently concerned with people, and so on. The process is taken a step further when later on in this chapter the seven broad areas of motivation are broken down yet again into combined areas of motivation.

First we focus on your highest peak of movitation. It is important that you attend to this most of all, because this is where you are likely to achieve your greatest satisfaction. Next we look at the major combinations of motivational areas and see what careers may be appropriate. You could well find yourself looking up three or even four areas having located our motivation in the matrix below.

*Primary areas of motivation*

|   | L | C | S | X | R | P | A |
|---|---|---|---|---|---|---|---|
| L | 1 |   |   |   |   |   |   |
| C |   | 2 |   |   |   |   |   |
| S |   |   | 3 |   |   |   |   |
| X |   |   |   | 4 |   |   |   |
| R |   |   |   |   | 5 |   |   |
| P |   |   |   |   |   | 6 |   |
| A |   |   |   |   |   |   | 7 |

## Literary

ou are attracted by careers involving words, ideas and
ommunication. You will be happy reading or writing a lot –
robably both. Other interests or activities might also appeal,
ut these can be saved for leisure time. It is with a literary
ctivity that you want to spend most of your time.

You probably have some background or experience in this
rea already. Your favourite subject at school may well have
een English or something closely related to it, such as history.
he lessons you enjoyed most were those in which you
onstructed essays or had a chance to write creatively. You
ave probably written a few short stories at some time in your
fe or tried your hand at poetry. Words fascinate you and you
njoy knowing their meanings as well as using them precisely.

If you have not been engaged in literary events hitherto, it
 possible that your self-awareness has changed. Perhaps now
 the time to find out whether you have any talent. Some
eople have produced a first novel after retirement.

As well as the specifically 'literary' careers there are other

associated careers which are easier to get into. Very few of u
can expect to be great poets but we may reasonably expect t
be wordsmiths of some kind.

Some careers in this area do depend on exceptional talent
for example, those of author, poet and dramatist. But succes
in these areas rarely just happens; it often requires years c
practice as well as the ability to cope with failure. Other career
depend much more upon academic qualifications. At th
professional level, a certain amount of specialised study is likel
to be a requirement (as in the case of librarian or journalist). I
you can combine your literary motivation with another ther
are careers at all levels, particularly in the administrative are
There are more opportunities to work with words in everyda
administration and communication than in the area of literar
aesthetics.

*Careers*

| | |
|---|---|
| actor/actress | language teacher |
| editor | librarian |
| historian | literary critic |
| interpreter | novelist |
| journalist | proof reader |

## 2. Creative

You want a career in which you can express yourself creativel
but not with words so much as in music or some form of fin
art. Your medium is visual or oral as opposed to verbal. Beaut
and aesthetics are your passions.

Many people are attracted by careers in this area becaus
they sound exciting. The opportunity to express ourselves ha
a universal appeal, though comparatively few can make a livin
from art – at least in its purest forms. But we like the sound c
the creative lifestyle, with its overtones of Bohemianism an
iconoclasm. The discipline actually to be a successful artist i
another thing altogether, especially when the audience w
would like to applaud us remains unappreciative!

Do you have the talent? What evidence is there? The abilit
tests are less helpful in this area because success will depen

pon popular taste and fashion rather than specific mental ptitudes; it is hard to set an examination in creative potential. popular music, a feel for what many people will enjoy stening to is the key, whereas a formal scholarship from a usic school carries no guarantee of success.

Maybe you feel that your budding talent was never eveloped at school and was stifled later when you have to put he need to earn a living first. It is probably easier to start late ith art than music, though there are few rules in this area; etermination and a belief in yourself are the essential rerequisites.

There are few opportunities for those who want to live olely by presenting their own work. You will need to be repared to sacrifice income as well as security on a full-time asis. There is more stability in a design team, or in an rchestra, as a member of the theatre or TV production team. ou may be able to compromise without sacrificing your leals. Do you need to make your own 'statement' or can you e content giving people what they enjoy? For example, you ould apply your art in such areas as the practical – thus naking it into a craft, or in the social – by becoming a teacher. self-expression is essential and you would be discontent sing your art to provide a service rather than presenting it for s own sake, the following are some of the few opportunities pen to you:

*areers*

| | |
|---|---|
| rchitect | interior designer |
| rtist | make-up artist |
| ancer | musician |
| ressmaker | sculptor |
| ngraver | silversmith |
| orist | vision mixer |
| oldsmith | window dresser |
| lustrator | |

## Social

our main interest lies in helping or assisting others. You are keen to see them develop, improve themselves and becom self-reliant. You are prepared to subordinate your own wishe to the service of others. It is not simply a question of being wit people – there are lots of careers in which you might be mor popular – but of viewing the needs of others as the end produc of your work.

How well and in what ways do you develop relationship with others? Have you an obviously caring nature, seeing you own reward in the natural enjoyment and benefit other derive from your attention? Or perhaps you are a mor detached type with some need to do something for other without getting too personally involved. Nearly all the soci careers have some kind of emotional involvement. If you feelings are easily bruised it may be better to give this area miss. A strong personality is often required just in order t cope and it may take a thicker skin than you realise.

It is sensible to get some experience before taking up a caree in this area. In the ordinary way there is very little availabl provided to help you to make up your mind. Your schoolday were largely intended to develop you scholastically – vocation training related to social service is unlikely to have had a plac important thought it may be. Have you enjoyed babysitting Have you been an assistant at a summer camp, a scoutmaste or guide leader, a voluntary helper or a prison visitor? If so, yo are on the right lines.

There are lots of careers in the social area as so many of th nation's resources are devoted to education, training, healt and welfare programmes. Some jobs require extensive train ing as well as natural interpersonal skills: you need profes sional qualifications for social work, teaching and almost all th jobs in which responsibility for others is directly dependen upon your judgement. We expect our general practitioners t be highly competent. The more the job becomes advisory or c an assisting nature as opposed to influential and controllin the less essential the qualifications.

*Careers*

| | |
|---|---|
| ambulance crew | chiropodist |
| careers adviser | doctor |

| educational psychologist | osteopath |
| health visitor | physiotherapist |
| hostel warden | probation officer |
| industrial nurse | remedial teacher |
| midwife | social worker |
| nurse | teacher (infant/junior) |
| nursery nurse | |

## 4. Executive

You are motivated by activities in which you can organise and influence others. You will want to have responsibility for managing others as well as making decisions about what should be done and how it should be done.

Some executive responsibility can be found in many careers, but if this kind of motivation is a distinctive feature you are clearly ambitious. For example, you are likely to be pushy and even aggressive at times in order to get what you want. If your motivation peak is very high you are unlikely to be content as 'second in command'. You will want to see some tangible evidence of your success in getting to the top and therefore material rewards are very important to you.

Even though our educational system is both extensive and highly structured, people who pursue careers in the executive area are not necessarily academic or even highly qualified; success depends a good deal upon hard-to-define qualities such as a flair and initiative.

Do you have experience of spotting opportunities, particularly for making some extra money, and then making something of them? People with this motivation don't wait for things to happen – they make them happen. You might have any kind of background and any kind of talent: you could be an executive in a creative area such as film making, or an administrative area such as banking, or in numerous others. The essential characteristic of this motivation is the will to succeed, wherever you find yourself. Thus, if your background is in research, you may see an opportunity to exploit your research commercially; if you are in welfare administration, you may feel you might do better for yourself in the private sector.

*Careers*

| | |
|---|---|
| business consultant | personnel director |
| export salesman | political agent |
| management consultant | politician |
| managing director | retail manager |
| marketing manager | sales manager |
| negotiator | team manager |

## 5. Research

This attraction shows how much you enjoy acquiring knowledge. As a result of this you seem prepared to devote a great deal of time to study and the careers which appeal to you generally need academic, professional or special qualifications. It is likely that you are curious about why things happen as they do. You do not like making guesses – you like to find reasons. You enjoy applying facts and arriving at solutions through logic and analytical investigation.

At school, you would have preferred scientific subjects, particularly the mainstream disciplines of mathematics, physics, chemistry and biology. You will have enjoyed objective problem solving and being able to sift through information in order to draw conclusions. You will have enjoyed experimenting and working with formulae.

Many people admire the intellectual rigour required in careers connected with research, and it is not everyone who possesses the patience and discipline to do well. These careers are difficult to take up as second careers since most training follows directly from subjects studied at school. Again, the demands of the training are such that it is preferable to undertake it before other responsibilities, such as a family, make study more difficult. There is also some justification to the theory that the best researchers do their most important work – make their breakthrough – in their early twenties.

The pursuit of a career in this area inevitably makes you into something of a specialist. There are few opportunities for general scientists, although some people have made a living by writing popular books which explain various scientific theories to lay people in an interesting way. Generally, you will need to be able to sustain an interest in a narrow part of science, possibly within the same institution or with the same employer for most of your career. The country is crying out for more scientists and technologists, though the areas of demand do change, for example, computer science is currently more in demand than geology. As in any field, the top jobs are always highly competitive.

*Careers*

| | |
|---|---|
| astronomer | material scientist |
| bacteriologist | mathematician |
| botanist | meteorologist |
| chemist | microbiologist |
| dietitian | ophthalmist |
| ergonomist | physicist |
| experimental psychologist | radiographer |
| forensic scientist | surgeon |
| laboratory technician | |

## 6. Practical

Motivation in this area shows that you want to be up and doing. By contrast, a sedentary career is likely to have little appeal: it would confine you or give you too little opportunity to actually make something. In fact there are two strong elements to a practical motivation, and it is possible to have one without the other and still get a high score on the questionnaire.

The first is that you may want to be out and about as well as physically involved, so that labour of some kind might be involved. The second element is the need to work with your hands, whether in a rugged or a precise and highly skilled way. In either case, you probably enjoy touching materials and constructing objects. You may have a technical or craft interest and at times this can approach the artistic. Although you may be less obviously a craftsman you will still enjoy being active and mobile and you will no doubt take pride in the employment of physical skills.

How good are you with your hands? Do you enjoy intricate

operations or working on a large scale? Some natural talent or affinity with materials or the environment is often detectable at an early age. Do you like shaping, cutting, or moulding with wood or clay? Or do you prefer engines and equipment?

Whether you work with natural or artificial materials, whether your interest is in a craft or simply in being active, there are opportunities at all levels. Some careers have years of study as a prerequisite whereas others depend upon experience and polished manual dexterity. A sure eye and a careful pair of hands might be enough for some, while others require a theoretical understanding as well.

A distinctive feature of careers in this area is the isolation which often characterises them: the forester, the driver and the diver work largely alone. Other careers may still require individual skills but also involve co-ordinating individual efforts with those of others in a productive team effort. A number of the craft skills relating to the building trade fall into this category.

*Careers*

animal keeper
blacksmith/farrier
boat builder
builder
butcher
carpenter
coastguard
cook
diver
driver
farmer
fireman
fisherman
fitter
forester
gamekeeper
groom
groundsman

guard
gunsmith
instrument maker
jockey
joiner
lighthouse keeper
lock keeper
locksmith
mechanic
merchant seaman
miner
nature conservancy warden
oil rig worker
shipping pilot
traffic warden
upholsterer
veterinary nurse

# 7. Administrative

This is a broad area of motivation covering business finance and office administration. It has to do with the running of an organisation whether a private enterprise or a public institution, and involves the organisation of people, resources and information.

To be successful you need to be orderly and systematic, though not in the same way as the scientist; your goal is to be an organiser, co-ordinator and adviser in a commercial setting, however loosely that may be defined. Administrators 'know what is going on' within the organisation and they make information available to those who need it. They rarely make strategic policy decisions themselves. You will know the value of qualifications and hence your own market worth. It is rare for people to succeed in large organisations unless they have the recognised qualifications of the relevant professional institute: insurance requires insurance exams, banking requires banking exams, accounting requires accounting exams and so on. It is possible to work your way up within an organistion but increasingly it seems preferable to extend one's education before embarking upon a professional career. For example, professional accountants have recently found themselves at a disadvantage when competing for jobs against accountants who also possess a degree.

Administration as an activity is changing since it now frequently requires people-related skills (the 'over-the-counter' manner) or different technical skills (eg computer literacy). Nevertheless, the key motivation is the same as for a career connected with some aspect of financial, legal, commercial or business organisation. High-level administrative jobs involve running large organisations and there are many types of work available in banking, insurance and economics as well as in all areas of business.

*Careers*

| | |
|---|---|
| accountant | administrator |
| accounting technician | auditor |
| actuary | bank clerk |

bookkeeper
building society manager/
   assistant
bursar
cashier
clerk
company secretary

industrial relations officer
legal executive
purser
records clerk
securities analyst
tax inspector

## Combined patterns of motivation

A distinct peak of motivation will show you where your major direction lies but a secondary or even third peak may reveal a key emphasis you would like to see in your work. In fact, although your own motivation may be very clear, it is rare to find a career that does not contain several elements. This is where matching yourself to a career becomes more complicated, but it need not be difficult if you take the structured approach we use in this book. It is as well to read not only the major patterns of motivation but also the combinations given below. In this way, you can think about extremes of possibilities and then narrow these down until you get the correct focus.

*Combined areas of motivation*

|   | L | C | S | X | R | P | A |
|---|---|---|---|---|---|---|---|
| **L** | 1 |   |   |   |   |   |   |
| **C** | 8 | 2 |   |   |   |   |   |
| **S** | 14 | 9 | 3 |   |   |   |   |
| **X** | 19 | 15 | 10 | 4 |   |   |   |
| **R** | 23 | 20 | 16 | 11 | 5 |   |   |
| **P** | 26 | 24 | 21 | 17 | 12 | 6 |   |
| **A** | 28 | 27 | 25 | 22 | 18 | 13 | 7 |

## Creative and literary

This combination shows motivation careers with an intellectual content. Your interest will primarily be for ideas rather than for material things. You will want to have an outlet for personal expression and to work in an imaginative or creative environment. This does not necessarily mean a rejection of reality, only that the emphasis of your work should be aesthetic.

In fact, careers in this area may range from the almost totally aesthetic to the high-gloss 'media' jobs. Your personal direction will be influenced by how much of your remaining motivation tends towards the executive or the administrative.

*Careers*

actor/actress
advertising copywriter
dramatist

film reviewer
TV production assistant

## 9. Social and creative

This combination of preferences brings together sensitivity towards art and a caring relationship with others. Work in this area demands patience, tact and emotional warmth. In careers requiring this combination art will generally take second place to the social requirement; it is used as a means or technique for helping, not as an end in itself.

There are few opportunities available and those which do exist are not very highly paid. In fact, much of the work in this area is done on a part-time or voluntary basis. A good deal of selflessness is required; you will also need organising ability, though executive and administrative motivation are not likely to feature highly. Some practical motivation may often appear as well. These jobs are for people who want to use their skill in a caring environment for the welfare of others. They may be involved in improving a person's physical co-ordination or mental health as well as with artistic appreciation and eductional development.

*Careers*

art therapist

music therapist

nursery teacher

occupational therapist

## 10. Social and executive

If you have this combination of preferences then you obviously have a need to work with people. This is less likely to be in a caring or obviously helping relationship than in business or administrative management. You will probably prefer the business to the public sector, though this is not always so. Your preferences for working with, and almost definitely through, people will be even clearer if at the same time you reject areas of work in which you would be in contact with things, objects, numbers or ideas.

Those with this combination should be socially skilled and usually they are: make sure these preferences do not arise simply because you would like to have talents that in fact you do not possess! Careers in this area are generally for people with a background of social service who want more influence and who enjoy managing or organising.

*Careers*

director of social services

funeral director

head teacher of large school

hotel manager

job interviewer

retail manager

salesperson

## 11. Executive and research

This is an unusual combination of preferences which are often thought to be mutually exclusive. People who hold one set do not usually hold the other. It is the association of the intellectual in direct juxtaposition with the commercial that is apparently so odd. If you have pursued a career with a research bias you have followed a course of study and will have denied yourself personal gain of a material or political kind. Most research careers are directed towards coming up with information of some kind. They therefore constitute a back-up expert service which is commercially exploited by those whose

motivation is inherently of a different kind. The commerciali-
sation of science is an expensive business; there are few
opportunities to simply 'start up' on your own. Recently there
has been a growth in computer-related businesses, which are
often started up at relatively little cost. However, it is much
more difficut to start up a new business in one of the
traditional sciences. One of the problems businesses have is to
identify the entrepreneurs with a technical/scientific background – so if you have these preferences, you could well be a
valuable property!

*Careers*

director of private research
   or scientific enterprise
dispensing optician
general chemist

manager of computer bureau
medical representative
technical representative
veterinary surgeon

## 12. Research and practical

If this is your combination, you will enjoy the application of
science. Research will be empty theory, merely cold abstrac-
tion, unless it can be brought to bear on some physical problem
and achieve something. You may well work with people and a
business but your interest is with the equipment and technology. You will be scientific, but will also enjoy working skilfully
with your hands. You like to see things happen, to produce
concrete end results. There could also be a preference for
activity – you like to get out and about and see science at work
in the environment. There are few careers for which study
and professional status are not prerequisites.

*Careers*

agriculturalist
bio medical engineer
computer engineer
engineer
environmental health officer
ergonomist
geologist
horologist

hydrologist
metallurgist
navigating officer
scientific instrument maker
surveyor
technologist
work study officer

## 13. Practical and administrative

Is it possible to be at the same time active and involved in office work? Careers which are normally considered sedentary appear to be incompatible with those connected with handling materials and equipment. Usually it can only be managed, if at all, by some kind of 'trade off' arrangement, such as spending 50 per cent or thereabouts of your time in each environment. Thus you may go out to do your work and then return to your office to compile a report. It is often the case that people in these careers view the administrative side as the 'necessary evil' because their hearts are more passionately located in the practical and active elements of their work.

*Careers*

agricultural secretary
baths manager
builder's merchant
customs officer
manufacturing superintendent
office machinery mechanic
organisation and methods officer
rating valuation officer
storekeeper

## 14. Literary and social

This pattern shows a desire for a career combining the opportunity to help others with some involvement in ideas. It may be a case of transmitting ideas to others with the aim of enlightening them or of encouraging them to communicate and express themselves in their own right. Most jobs have a connection with teaching and usually demand some expert skill with languages, either of an oral or written kind – often both. The emphasis, whether literary or social, varies in different jobs: the art form or literary subject may be the principal attraction and this will define the social forum, which could be a class meeting together for literary appreciation or to learn a language. Alternatively, language or a related subject may be used as an aid to the mental development and emotional capability of others, as in so many forms of teaching and therapy.

*Careers*

interviewer speech therapist
language teacher training officer
liberal studies teacher

## 15. Creative and executive

So you want to be involved with art and make money too? It seems that life is going to be varied and exciting whatever your values and ideals. You will want a stimulating and expressive environment but you also require some recognisable signs of material success. You will enjoy the elaborate expression of ideas even though they may be temporary. You will be concerned with style and with novelty. You will be competitive and enjoy taking risks, preferring careers where the demands are continually changing or where there is always a sensational element. You will therefore reject routine activities and you want to make your own decisions on key issues. People with this kind of motivation are often opinionated and prefer to leave details, as well as facts and figures, to others. They regard themselves as self-starters and often leave the 'finishing off' to other people. It is possible that you will be inspired and will often be able to persuade others; you will enjoy having influence and converting others to your tastes.

*Careers*

advertising account brand manager
 executive fashion buyer
art dealer media director

## 16. Social and research

The application of scientific knowledge and techniques in the service of others is what appeals to you. Although you have plenty of contact with other people your expertise will keep you detached and your role will often be advisory. Your assistance to others is therefore much more likely to be of a material or informational kind rather than of a qualitative type involving any great degree of direct emotional input. You will require personal skills, such as tact and understanding, though

**147**

you are unlikely to maintain a continually caring involvement. You will have a record of success with analytical and statistical subjects but are probably too outgoing to be content with pure research work. However, the emphasis, as the examples below show, varies widely.

*Careers*

| | |
|---|---|
| clinical psychologist | orthoptist |
| dental assistant | radiographer |
| dentist | science teacher |
| nurse | social science researcher |

## 17. Executive and practical

You want to be involved with administration and commerce but without being confined to an office. Though office work of some kind is likely to be necessary, you will not often be found behind the desk. Rather, you will be out of doors viewing, estimating or managing on site. There are a number of entrepreneurial activities relating to the land and agricultural products as well as careers in property and equipment. You may be involved in running a large enterprise such as an estate or alternatively you could be a one-man-band. It is usual to combine education with practical experience and there is no point in thinking of careers in these areas unless you can turn your hand to most things, fixing them yourself or getting them going. You will need to be enterprising as well as able to recognise the value of commodities and materials.

*Careers*

| | |
|---|---|
| accident assessor | production manager |
| auctioneer | publican |
| demonstrator | transport manager |
| estate agent | undertaker |
| farm manager | |

## 18. Research and administrative

This combination would involve you with facts and figures. You will want to deal with information and your approach to problem solving will be systematic and logical. The pattern is particularly clear when little value is set upon the people-related or more intuitive areas of motivation. Thus you will want to deal with data, applying analytical methods in administrative and commercial settings.

You are very well placed if you have these preferences. There has recently been an expansion of office systems which is fortunate for you! Indeed in some areas, the technocrat appears to be superseding conventional roles. For example, in banking, computer experts are now obtaining senior posts where once only years of banking experience would have sufficed. You may be sought after as an expert providing back-up services. If you have entrepreneurial motivation as well, then perhaps some 'leading edge' information technology business would suit you – there is such a demand that many have started up. If you also have a welfare interest look for opportunities in areas of training.

*Careers*

| | |
|---|---|
| business systems analyst | operational researcher |
| computer programmer | statistician |
| economist | systems analyst |
| market researcher | |

## 19. Literary and executive

This combines an interest in ideas and communication with the chance of exploiting these in business. There may be a specific involvement in books or at least with the spoken or written word. You may be keen on writing yourself and will certainly be very appreciative of it. It is difficult to have a career in this area without a background in media, which often follows an academic background. Your studies are likely to have been in literature, languages, history, law or related areas. The careers which attract you are highly competitive and frequently demanding of the highest intellectual as well as entrepreneurial skills. Few opportunities exist at anything but the highest levels. Sometimes these preferences are combined with administration, which shows a leaning more towards the business organisation side. If on the other hand your bias is towards the creative it will show that the thrust of your interest is more intellectually driven.

*Careers*

| | |
|---|---|
| conference executive | public relations manager |
| literary agent | publisher |
| newspaper editor/manager | radio or TV producer |

## 20. Creative and research

You are unlikely to be able to pursue your motivation with this combination unless you have both skill and training, which can be either from the artistic or scientific side. You want to combine the two in your career and this makes you unusual, because these areas are often thought to be mutually exclusive. However, art can be close to engineering – for example in car styling, as in so many other manufacturing operations. Many fine artists employed in the restoration of pictures need to know about chemical processes as well as about physics.

*Careers*

| | |
|---|---|
| beautician | medical illustrator |
| cartographer | museum assistant |
| designer | photographer |
| draughtsman | restorer |
| lighting technician | |

## 21. Social and practical

Your interest is in people and you will want to do something for them which is practical and shows definite results. The environment you are in as well as the skills you possess enable you to be active. The pattern is more clearly defined if you reject the administrative areas of work as being too desk-bound for you. You may well be a good organiser but you like to carry things out and see them done so that in contrast with your practical management, your desk might be untidy and the paperwork forgotten. Your background might be in sports or you may have an artistic inclination. The 'people' content of

he work varies a good deal, verging on the instructional at one
nd to the therapeutic at the other. But in the end it is an
nterest in people rather than the activity itself which will
nake you successful in these areas of work.

*Careers*

| | |
|---|---|
| hairdresser | prison officer |
| masseur/masseuse | sports centre assistant |
| occuptional therapist | team coach |
| police officer | youth leader |

## 2. Executive and administrative

Success in this area often depends upon having a skills
background in, for example, banking, insurance, commerce or
office administration. The skills are taken further than would
be required in a purely technical job because they will be used
in management and business decision-making. If you combine
these preferences, you have a powerful drive to succeed in the
business world. Possibly, artistic or welfare-related areas are
less important to you as you will want to concern yourself with
the 'real world'. Success depends largely upon your own
efforts but the skills you have will help you get there – which
in your case will be to the top! Your technical knowledge and
professional background will make you a formidable force in
the boardroom as you enter general management from a
functional specialism. However, you will have a tendency to
make decisions on the basis of evidence from the figures, and
the 'commercial' side of business will interest you more than
the outward-facing or media-related areas.

*Careers*

| | |
|---|---|
| bank manager | insurance agent |
| broker | office manager |
| club manager | sales administrator |
| estate manager | tax consultant |
| film producer | turf accountant |
| finance director | underwriter |

## 23. Literary and research

You may be able to combine these preferences in a career which fuses science with art. In this case, you are likely to be highly qualified: you will be one of the lucky few who are very highly specialised and for whom there are careers available. Most careers will be in an academic or educational environment. If your background is in research you may also have literary talent which allows you to write about your subject. Additional personal skills would be required if you are to be successful in presenting your work to others as a lecturer or trainer.

*Careers*

anthropologist
archaeologist
information scientist

science writer
technical writer

## 24. Creative and practical

These preferences come together more harmoniously than most. You will enjoy the practical arts where design and beauty can be employed in a useful way. This may be as additional decoration to materials or as an intrinsic part of the material or product itself. Your interests verge closely upon craft activities but are distinguished from them because they are utilitarian although, admittedly, crafts often have a beauty of their own.

The activities which interest you are often practised in isolation or within a group of like-minded people. They are not social or material so you will probably reject those areas which connect you with commerce. You may occasionally be able to see a way of combining your motivation with teaching or in some form of business. There is rarely a career structure and much depends upon whether you have both the skill and a definite idea of the life-style which would satisfy you.

*Careers*

book-binder
cabinet maker

cameraman
confectioner

| | |
|---|---|
| resser | gardener |
| mbalmer | jewellery maker |
| mbroiderer | pattern cutter |
| ngineering pattern maker | picture framer |
| lm projectionist | potter |
| yman | |

## 5. Social and administrative

Nork in which the object is to help others appeals to you but ou will want to bring together resources to make this happen. Although you may have a caring temperament yourself, your reference is to arrange services rather than get involved in a irect way. You are often a supplies officer helping those in the ront line, such as teachers or social workers for example. You vill want to administer a system which provides people with esources. In this area of work it is often difficult to satisfy thers, and indeed you may have to reconcile yourself to the act that you cannot always help personally: you will only get nvolved as far as is legally or contractually permitted. However, cases where personal judgement is required occur requently and you will gain satisfaction from knowing and pplying the system to the benefit of others.

*Careers*

| | |
|---|---|
| ourier/local representative | medical secretary |
| mployment officer | principal nursing officer |

## 26. Literary and practical

These two preferences do not combine easily in one career: vhen you think about it, it is difficult to see how writing and being active can take place at the same time! You have to leave one before you can do the other. It may in fact be the case that you will reconcile this by having two quite separate careers. Alternatively, one may simply have to be left to your leisure ime – and which one will in the end be determined by the stronger preference.

If you want a career with this combination, you will probably have to follow one or the other preference and then transpose it into the alternative setting. To give some exam ples, an agricultural secretary does the same work as other secretaries but is out and about more in the country; a printer has a mechanical and increasingly technical job where the en product is words (although he does not need to be 'literary' a such).

*Careers*

agricultural secretary       technical writer
printer

## 27. Creative and administrative

You may be creative in your own right but need to be a good organiser and aware of costs to do your job effectively; you may have a background in office work but want to be part of a creative enterprise. Your job might be of the type which provides back-up or support to others, but in some cases you might have to take a leading role. Thus, a chef has a good dea of decision making, as does a merchandiser.

*Careers*

chef                          studio assistant
choreographer's assistant     theatre administrator
cinema manager                theatre box office clerk
merchandiser                  wardrobe manager

## 28. Literary and administrative

This combination directs you towards many possible careers It relates to those which are largely to do with communication where the emphasis is upon figures, and is often a haven for people whose initial interest and background or training was literary, but who came to the conclusion that business was likely to be a more rewarding environment for them. Alterna tively, for those with an administrative background the literary element gives wider opportunities. Careers range from executive to professional positions at all levels. There are opportunities in areas of public service, the private sector and the media. It is a very broad combination and you may need to study the rest of your motivational pattern to decide exactly where your emphasis should be.

*Careers*

administrator (clerical/
   executive)
barrister
company secretary
entertainments officer

legal executive
library assistant
secretary
solicitor
receptionist

## Chapter 5
# Taking Stock 2: Who I Will Become

Ability, personality and motivation all need to be considered in combination. It would be unwise to simply head off in the direction of what you most want to do without taking into account what you are most capable of doing, whether the job will continue to appeal and to what extent your personality will determine your success. There is little point in taking up a career which provides an intellectual challenge in the short term if your personality is of a type which enjoys making use of interpersonal skills or if you have an entrepreneurial drive towards success.

This book has given you three structured ways of analysing yourself and making deductions about your career: it is now time to put these structures together to form a realistic action plan. There may be some inconsistencies in the three structures which need to be resolved and your own life situation may mean that some compromises have to be made. For example, what do you do if your intellectual talent is greatest for numbers and you have low motivation for careers in administration or research? What if you like the idea of being a diver but appear to have no mechanical ability? And what if the idea of an outdoor occupation appeals to you but your experience since leaving school 20 years ago has been in banking? Whatever your particular circumstances and whatever the unique make-up of your intelligence, personality and motivation, the structured approach you have pursued through this book should guide you in the most logical way towards a suitable career.

We have found one simple overriding principle: use all your aptitudes to their maximum. Undersell yourself at your peril o if your aptitudes are high, don't deny them because you will eventually be bored. In general, the more you get on and do what you want to do and know what you can do, the happier and more respectful of yourself you will be.

## Case study 1: The ex-teacher

Amanda was 37. She had once been a teacher but left work in order to have a family. Now she was divorced and faced increasingly with the responsibility of providing for herself and her two children, one of whom was in senior school and the other well into junior school. Although she had worked for several successful years as a teacher before having a family, the idea of returning to teaching was unattractive. She had thought of herself as a good teacher but felt that the present-day demands on teachers would involve her much more in caring or social work, which she did not think she would be good at. The following was her summary of herself after she had tested her aptitudes:

|  | *least suitable* | *most suitable* |
|---|---|---|
| **Ability** | technical | analytical<br>numerical |
| **Personality** | aggressive<br>pushy | factual<br>sensitive |
| **Motivation** | persuasive | administrative<br>people<br>scientific |

Amanda was not surprised to find she had done well in the numerical and analytical tests because she had pursued sciences at school and had in fact been a biology teacher. It was her motivational results, showing a high preference for the administrative, which made her think of putting science to one side and moving into the administrative or office-based areas of work. She would still have the contact with people she enjoyed, though it looked as though she ought to avoid business in which she would have to be persuasive personally or sell herself. The quality of contact she should have with others was made clearer by the personality test results, which showed her to be rather more on the sensitive than the aggressive side. This was in tune with the way she thought of herself – as wanting to fit in with people rather than actually take charge of them. She felt she had a factual and matter-of-fact personality and it was this side of her that was probably attracted by administrative careers. Although there was some scientific motivation, she thought that what she liked about science was logic and being able to work in a systematic way, something which is clearly available in administration in the area of computers and office systems.

Amanda obtained a clerical job working in accounts and within a year had embarked upon accounting and administration courses at a local college in order to obtain qualifications in what she expects to be a satisfactory third career.

## Case study 2: The test engineer

Alan had qualifications in mechanics and electronics. He was the team leader, undertaking qualitative analysis and research studies of the company's products, in a large international organisation. Although his work had been interesting in the past and he had been told that it was highly valued by the company, he now felt that he was getting nowhere. Indeed, he still enjoyed the technology itself but he would have liked more say in what products were actually developed.

In addition, he felt that he would like more contact with the customers since he enjoyed the occasional but incidental contact he had with them as the technical expert. He had thought of leaving his present company and seeing if another might suit him better, but his wife was concerned about the impact that any relocation might have on their children's education and whether they could actually afford to move having recently taken on a large mortgage. These were his results on testing his aptitudes:

|  | *least suitable* | *most suitable* |
|---|---|---|
| **Ability** | acuity | technical<br>analytical |
| **Personality** |  | factual<br>group |
| **Motivation** | people<br>creative | persuasive<br>scientific<br>administrative |

Alan was interested to see that his personality was group-orientated. He enjoyed working with a team of people and in fact had on occasions been able to advise people who had come to him to discuss their personal difficulties. He had also liked joining social groups, but had had more opportunity for this outside than inside work. In fact, he began to wonder whether it might have been the lack of management opportunity at work that was beginning to frustrate him.

A further area of frustration was clarified when he saw that his motivational results included both a persuasive and an administrative interest as well as the scientific one that he had expected. This also indicated that he wanted more managerial responsibility in making decisions and influencing matters. The administrative interest made him think of a commercial as opposed to a purely technical role. It was clear that he wanted to change his career within the organisation although the lack of any strong creative motivation seemed to indicate that a radical move into a different function, such as marketing or public relations, was unnecessary.

In fact, he persuaded his company to give him some experience in the area of service engineering. This allowed him to apply his knowledge in a practical way and gain some experience of the commercial world, as well as meeting customers. The job demanded skills he had never used before but which had always been dormant and he found he was able to extend his career in new and challenging ways. After a short time in which his career appeared to stand still because he had made a lateral rather than a vertical move, his career accelerated and he obtained a management role.

## Case study 3: The college leaver

Joe had enjoyed obtaining a degree in Pure Mathematics. He had felt intellectually stimulated at university which he liked for all its aspects, including the social side. He had not only been a keen member of a sports team but had also participated in a debating society and was a leading light on the students' committee. He was uncertain what to do, although he had been offered a research post at the university which would not only pay him but lead on to a higher degree. However, he had a feeling that he had been too long a student and felt a hankering for the real world. Amid pressure from his parents, who were justly proud of him, and the expectations of his tutors he saw no credible alternative until he tested his aptitudes:

|  | *least suitable* | *most suitable* |
|---|---|---|
| **Ability** | acuity technical | analytical numerical verbal |
| **Personality** | sensitive | factual aggressive group |
| **Motivation** | scientific people | persuasive administrative creative |

Joe's aptitudes were good but he saw little chance to use his verbal ability if he stayed in the academic world, except as a teacher or perhaps a writer. He felt he wanted to break away from the university environment and that his strong verbal bility held the promise of a job where communication and dealing with people would play a large rather than just an occasional part. The personality results showed a lively, aggressive and group-orientated personality which made him think that he might find university life confining. The strongest evidence came from his motivational results: the emphasis here was not related to mathematics or science but much more to a job in which he might be involved with organisations. It seemed clear that he had ambitions and wanted a life-style that he would not find in a purely academic career.

Looking through the lists of opportunities corresponding to his summary pattern, the idea of marketing appealed strongly. He then reflected that he had once considered studying economics rather than mathematics, and this might have been more relevant to his interest in politics and business. With marketing as a career, he could make use of all his logical and numerical talents but have plenty of chance to draw them out working with others and making decisions in a challenging and varied commercial environment. He decided to go to business school and take a degree in Business Administration. He joined a large company as a graduate trainee gaining general experience until he joined the marketing department. He hopes to become director of marketing of a sizeable company or alternatively run his own business one day.

## Case study 4: The reluctant social worker

Marie was a residential social worker at a local school for the physically handicapped. She had worked part time there while still at school and had been offered a job when she left at 16. She did not have enough qualifications to go on to become a qualified social worker. She was now 22 and beginning to think about where her career should go. Although she quite enjoyed life at the school she felt herself getting increasingly irritated by the 'systems'. She also felt that her life generally was not developing; the residential aspect of her life meant that she worked very unsociable hours.

On completing the tests, she obtained the following results:

|  | *least suitable* | *most suitable* |
|---|---|---|
| **Ability** | technical | numerical<br>verbal |
| **Personality** | group | lively<br>aggressive |
| **Motivation** | literary<br>research | social<br>executive |

She did better on the ability tests than she had expected but still not well enough to make further academic study easy. She did best on the numerical and verbal reasoning ((she admitted to having quite enjoyed school although she hadn't taken it particularly seriously).

More surprising to Marie were her personality results. She had always seen herself as a group member with a fairly placid approach to life. The results, however, suggested that she was actually lively and aggressive and this was why she was finding the regimented approach of the school increasingly difficult to cope with. She was not particularly group-orientated although she was by no means a loner. This also fitted in with her feelings of never having a private life.

The pattern suggested that she needed opportunities to initiate activity and be a great deal more directive in her approach. The motivation results suggested that while she enjoyed contact with other people, she also wanted a little more 'business'-type activity in which she could employ a more persuasive approach and see some end results of her labours.

When her results were combined and various opportunities explored it became obvious that Marie was more suited to employment in which she could provide a service to others but have considerably more say, and where her lively and cheerful approach would be of benefit. Some kind of self-employment was also explored. On looking closely at the opportunities available locally, she decided to move into the retail trade getting a job in a small specialist health food shop (a general nterest of hers for some years) where the local owner was ooking for a new assistant who could ultimately manage the shop on his behalf.

The change to a retail environment liberated Marie and her friends commented on how much happier she seemed. After six months the shop owner had enough confidence in her approach and knowledge of the products to allow her to manage the shop, with very successful results.

## Putting it all together

### Summary chart

Write in below the vital descriptions of yourself as they have appeared from the three areas of analysis you have worked through.

|  | *least suitable* | *most suitable* |
|---|---|---|
| **Ability** | | |
| **Personality** | | |
| **Motivation** | | |

## Myself as I am now

*Regarding how successful I feel with my career right now, this is how I would rate myself:*

**poor** |———|———|———|———|———|———|———| **wonderful**
0    1    2    3    4    5    6    7

*This is how I look:*

_____

_____

_____

*This is what I own:*

_____

_____

_____

*This is how I feel about myself:*

_____

_____

_____

*People I know say these things about me:*

_____

_____

_____

*I can describe how I feel about my present occupation using these words:*

_____

_____

_____

_____

ossible careers suggested most strongly by my results

bilities

- _____
- _____
- _____

ersonality

- _____
- _____
- _____

lotivation

- _____
- _____
- _____

verall most suitable career(s) (That/Those which recur(s) lost often or with the strongest attraction)

- _____
- _____
- _____

*Is there anything which might prevent me from achieving my chosen career*

1. **Health**

_____

_____

2. **Circumstances**

_____

_____

3. **Lack of appropriate education**

_____

_____

4. **Age/experience**

_____

_____

5. **Present commitments**

_____

_____

6. **Risks**

_____

_____

7. **Other**

_____

_____

*Preparation*
Write a sentence in relation to each of the previous points (1–7) stating how the things which might prevent you will in fact be overcome.

1. _____
_____
_____

2. _____
_____
_____

3. _____
_____
_____

4. _____
_____
_____

5. _____
_____
_____

6. _____
_____
_____

7. _____
_____
_____

In order to obtain the career you want, write down first of all the necessary actions to be taken within the next week. Make out a second list for the actions you will have carried out within the next six months.

1.*Next week*

_____

_____

_____

_____

_____

_____

2.*Six months*

_____

_____

_____

_____

_____

_____

Write down the names of the key people who will influence or be affected by your career decisions. Write down as closely and as exactly as you can what they are likely to say.

| *Name* | *What will probably be said* |
|---|---|
| 1. _____<br>_____<br>_____ | _____<br>_____<br>_____ |
| 2. _____<br>_____<br>_____ | _____<br>_____<br>_____ |
| 3. _____<br>_____<br>_____ | _____<br>_____<br>_____ |
| 4. _____<br>_____<br>_____ | _____<br>_____<br>_____ |
| 5. _____<br>_____<br>_____ | _____<br>_____<br>_____ |

Write down your reaction to what might be said on the previous page.

1. _____

_____

_____

2. _____

_____

_____

3. _____

_____

_____

4. _____

_____

_____

5. _____

_____

_____

## Myself in a year's time

Think carefully about how you will be when you have obtained your career objectives or at least worked significantly towards them.

*This is how satisfied I feel with my career success:*

**poor** |———+———+———+———+———+———+———| **wonderful**
      0    1    2    3    4    5    6    7

*This is how I shall look:*

_____

_____

_____

*This is what I shall own:*

_____

_____

_____

*This is how I shall feel about myself:*

_____

_____

_____

*People I know will say these things about me:*

_____

_____

_____

*I will describe my occupation using these words:*

_____

_____

_____

_____

## Chapter 6

# Career Index

By this stage in the book you should have worked through the various ability tests, personality and motivation measures and have begun to pull all the information together. At each stage we have suggested many illustrative careers; the Career Index provides a further structured approach to matching your aptitudes with those most usually found in successful members of the career. This process is called 'trait matching'.

The aim is to match a person's individual aptitudes and disposition as closely as possible with those careers most likely to use and encourage them. This will give the individual the most scope for applying his or her skills. It is obvious that some careers demand a particular type of talent, and similarly, a person with a certain kind of personality or motivation may go further in one career than another. The idea of matching is a simple concept, but a great deal of research has been done on the techniques and information upon which it is based.

In a book of this nature, we can only talk about the type of career or broad career area rather than specific posts. Once you have narrowed down your field of search, more detailed advice on specific careers is freely available through the professional bodies, the library services and careers advisers.

You should also bear in mind that the nature of what a career actually involves tends to change as the world of work changes. Success in any job, however, depends first on possessing the appropriate set of basic abilities and then on other factors which are beyond the scope of this book. These could include the difficulty of getting to and from work; how well you get on with your peers and superiors; difficulties in the actual work environment; a certain amount of luck, eg if a position falls vacant at the right time, and so on.

The following list of over 400 careers is not exhaustive but should give you some idea of the range of possibilities.

## Using the Career Index

As you completed the tests and discovered your particular strengths and weaknesses, you will have noticed that each description of a trait was accompanied by some job examples. Most of these examples are to be found in the career index.

When you read the full entries, you will get a clearer picture of which careers are likely to suit you from all directions and which from only one or two directions. You should also look at the level of abilities. In some instances, there will be indicators to suggest that your particular personality or motivation could be a handicap even if you have the correct abilities. This process takes time but eventually you should begin to see which career areas seem most promising. You must then do more individual research, relating specific career requirements or opportunities to your personal circumstances.

Trait matching works because in any identifiable career, there is a type of person who is most usually successful. This is a stereotype. Within any career group, there will be a few people who do not totally conform to the stereotype, but as a general rule, the further you are from the stereotype the more difficult it is to be successful. The idea of this book is for you to follow your aptitudes and find a career which is going to suit you 'naturally', one in which you are most likely to be successful. It does not stop you trying any other career but if your abilities, personality and motivation are not suited to the job, you will have to bring something extra in order to be successful. So collect all your own information together, read the career index carefully and good hunting!

ACCIDENT ASSESSOR A very specialist role requiring a high level of general ability, an independent personality and motivational factors of an executive and practical nature.

ACCOUNTANT Well above average level of ability, particularly in numerical skills; factual and independent personality with administrative motivation. For management roles a more aggressive personality and executive motivation are useful.

ACCOUNTING TECHNICIAN Average to above average abilities, particularly in numerical and acuity; an FCPI personality and administrative motivation.

ACTOR Most levels of ability will find a 'slot' somewhere within the profession but a verbal strength is often helpful; aggressive and independent personality and a creative and literary motivational pattern is also useful, as is the need to combine confidence with sensitivity.

ACTUARY Well above average level of ability particularly numerical and acuity; FCPI personality with administrative motivation.

ADMINISTRATOR Variable level of ability dependent on levels of responsibility, but a joint verbal and numerical pattern required; calm and factual personality with administrative motivation.

ADVERTISING COPYWRITER Verbal abilities; sensitive personality with creative and literary motivational factors, together with considerable ambition in a very competitive environment.

ADVERTISING EXECUTIVE Variable abilities with an FLAG personality and creative and executive motivational factors.

AERONAUTICAL ENGINEER Well above average ability with strengths in numerical and technical; factual, calm and indeendent personality with a research and practical motivation attern.

AGENT (IMPORT/EXPORT) *see* IMPORT/EXPORT AGENT.

AGENT (SALES) Variable abilities and an FLAI personality. Variable motivation factors depending on area of operation, but practical and executive probably most useful.

AGRICULTURALIST Well above average ability, particularly in perceptual and analytical, are usually required for this laboratory-based career; also research and practical motivation. Personality is less precise, but normally factual, calm and independent advisable.

AGRICULTURAL MECHANIC Average to above average skills, particularly technical and numerical; factual personality with practical motivation and a liking for outdoor activity.

AGRICULTURAL SECRETARY *see* SECRETARY, but usually mobile.

AIR HOSTESS/STEWARD Variable abilities with an FLPG personality and practical and social motivation.

AIR TRAFFIC CONTROLLER Above average ability with strengths in the spatial and acuity areas; factual and calm personality with administrative motivation

AMBULANCE CREW Variable abilities with an FCPG personality and social motivation.

ANAESTHETIST Well above average ability with an analytical and perceptual bias; factual, calm and independent personality with research and administrative motivations.

ANIMAL KEEPER (ZOO or LABORATORY) Average all-round abilities usually with a fairly calm and independent personality and clear practical motivations. Very limited opportunities exist, so persistence is also required.

ANIMAL NURSE *see* ANIMAL KEEPER, VETERINARY NURSE

ANTHROPOLOGIST Well above average ability of a fairly general nature. Personality will vary according to the particular bias of the work; experimental, academic or literary. Normally more factual, sensitive and independent than group orientation. Literary and research motivations are usual.

ANTIQUE DEALER Variable levels of ability are found, normally with a bias towards numerical and spatial; personality is also variable depending on the type of establishment/practice but within the business field a factual and aggressive approach is valuable, together with practical and some executive interests.

ARBORIST Above to well above average ability, with a bias on spatial and technical skills; an SCPI personality with practical and research motivation.

ARCHAEOLOGIST Well above average abilities are normally fairly mixed; an independent personality and literary, research motivations needed for positions in a very competitive environment.

ARCHITECT Well above average ability specialising in numerical and spatial areas, with an SLAI personality and creative and practical motivation.

ARCHITECTURAL TECHNICIAN Average to above ability with a specialisation in technical and acuity skills and a calm personality.

ARCHIVIST Well above average ability, with verbal normally a strength. FCPI personality and research and administrative motivation.

ARMED FORCES OFFICER Average to above average ability without any strong specialisation; FCAG personality with social and some practical motivation.

ART DEALER Numerical and spatial abilities, usually with a factual and independent personality and creative, executive motivations.

ARTIST Average to above average ability for professional training and with definite sensitive, independent personality factors, creative motivation.

ART THERAPIST Above average general abilities with spatial specialisation; a sensitive, calm personality (often independent) with social and creative motivation.

ASTRONOMER Well above average numerical and perceptual abilities; factual and calm, independent personality with strong research motivation.

AUCTIONEER Variable abilities; FLAG personality and executive and practical motivation. The higher levels of ability are needed for professional qualifications.

AUDIOLOGY TECHNICIAN Above average ability, particularly numerical and technical; variable personality but usually factual and calm with practical and some research motivation.

AUDITOR Well above average ability, particularly numerical and analytical, with an FCPI personality and administrative motivation.

AUTHOR Variable abilities, an SLAI personality and literary motivation.

BACTERIOLOGIST Well above average ability, particularly perceptual and analytical; passive, factual and often independent personality with research and some practical motivation.

BAKER Technical and some perceptual ability, often with an independent and calm personality and practical motivation.

BALLET DANCER Variable abilities; SLAI personality and creative motivation, plus a great deal of hard work in the formative years.

BANK CLERK Above average ability, particularly in acuity and numerical skills; usually factual, passive and independent personality with administrative motivation.

BANK MANAGER Above average ability, with numerical and acuity uppermost; FCAP personality, administrative and executive motivation.

BAR PERSON Variable abilities; FLPG personality.

BARRISTER Above average verbal ability with some analytical; FCAI personality with literary and administrative motivation.

BEAUTICIAN Average ability, often with spatial and acuity strengths. An SLAG personality with creative and research motivation.

BILINGUAL SECRETARY Above average verbal ability and literary motivation. Personality will vary with the type of environment in which the secretary operates.

BIOLOGIST Well above average abilities particularly perceptual and analytical; passive, factual and often independent personality in research and some practical and research motivation.

BIOMEDICAL ENGINEER Well above average ability, with particular strengths in perceptual, spatial, technical. Variable personality depending on employment environment, with research and practical motivation.

BLACKSMITH/FARRIER Technical ability with factual and independent personality, often with an aggressive but calm approach; practical motivation.

BOAT BUILDER Variable abilities and personality but strongly practical motivation.

BOOK-BINDER Spatial and technical abilities together with a passive and independent personality and a creative and practical motivation.

BOOK CRITIC High verbal abilities with aggressive and independent personality and literary motivation.

BOOK ILLUSTRATOR Perceptual and spatial abilities; usually a sensitive and independent personality with creative motivation.

BOOKKEEPER Numerical and acuity abilities; factual and passive personality and administrative motivation.

BOOKMAKER *see* TURF ACCOUNTANT

BOOKSELLER Variable abilities but often high verbal and a clearly independent and often lively personality; executive and administrative motivation.

BOTANIST Well above average perceptual abilities; independent, passive personality and research interests for this usually laboratory-based area.

BREWER Perceptual and technical abilities, usually with a fairly independent personality and practical, research motivation.

BRICKLAYER Variable abilities but often technical skills, with a fairly aggressive and independent personality and highly practical motivation.

BROKER Above average numerical and analytical abilities; factual, aggressive personality with executive, administrative motivation and flair!

BUILDER'S MERCHANT Variable abilities and personality (often aggressive) with practical, administrative motivation.

BUILDING INSPECTOR Above average perceptual and technical abilities; factual, aggressive and independent personality and practical and administrative motivation.

BUILDING SOCIETY MANAGER/ASSISTANT Above average numerical and acuity abilities, variable personality and administrative motivation.

BUILDING SURVEYOR *see* SURVEYOR.

BURSAR Well above average numerical and acuity abilities, variable personality depending on employment area with administrative and sometimes executive motivations. Usually requires a specialist accounting qualification.

BUS CONDUCTOR Variable abilities with an FLPI and social and practical motivations.

BUS DRIVER Variable abilities, strongly independent personality and practical motivation.

BUSINESS CONSULTANT Above average ability with particular strengths in numerical and verbal; SCAI personality with executive motivation.

BUTCHER Variable abilities but often spatial strength; frequently an independent personality with practical motivation.

BUYER Average to above average numerical abilities, often with a spatial and technical supporting strength. An FLAI personality with creative and executive motivation.

CABINET MAKER Variable abilities (bias towards spatial and technical) and variable personality depending on employment environment, strongly creative and practical motivation.

CAMERAMAN Above average technical ability with factual and calm personality; creative and practical motivations.

CAREERS ADVISER Above average general ability, calm and independent personality and social motivations, together with a liking for adolescents.

CARPENTER Variable abilities, but often with bias towards spatial and technical areas and strongly practical motivation. Personality will vary according to the employment environment.

CARTOGRAPHER Well above average ability (particularly spatial) and some numerical skills, with a factual, independent and usually calm personality and creative and research motivations.

CASHIER Often above average ability, particularly in acuity and/or numerical areas, usually fairly passive, group personality with administrative motivation.

CHEF/COOK Variable abilities, often with spatial strengths; FLPI personality and practical, creative and administrative motivation, together with the ability to work unsociable hours.

CHEMIST Well above average perceptual and analytical abilities combine with research motivation.

CHIMNEY SWEEP Variable abilities with an increasingly technical bias; FLPI personality and practical motivation.

CHIROPODIST Above average general ability, calm and independent personality with social motivation.

CHOREOGRAPHER Variable ability and personality is often sensitive and lively, with a creative and administrative motivation and considerable determination.

CINEMA MANAGER Variable abilities, with numerical and acuity skills often predominating, a balanced personality (but often independent and sometimes aggressive) with creative and administrative motivation.

CIVIL ENGINEER Well above average abilities, particularly in numerical and technical areas with a factual, independent personality, often with some aggressive tendencies, and practical and executive motivations.

CIVIL SERVANT Variable levels of ability, depending on the level of aspiration; personality will vary with the various departments and working environments but frequently factual, passive and group factors predominate, together with strong administrative motivation.

CLERK Acuity abilities predominate, with administrative interests, but personality varying with the employment environment.

CLINICAL PSYCHOLOGIST Well above average ability, frequently with perceptual and analytical strengths. Factual, calm and independent personality most usual, together with social and research motivation.

CLUB MANAGER Variable abilities with an FLAG personality and executive and administrative motivation.

COASTGUARD Variable abilities with a factual and independent personality and practical interests; follows a sea-going first career.

COMMUNITY SOCIAL WORKER Very similar to community warden, but with more variety in personality and at the social activity level.

COMMUNITY WARDEN Variable abilities, an SCPG personality with social and practical motivation.

COMPANY SECRETARY Well above average ability, with particular verbal and numerical strengths; factual, calm and independent personality with a literary and administrative motivation.

COMPOSITOR Spatial and technical abilities, a factual, calm personality and literary and practical motivation.

COMPUTER ENGINEER Well above average numerical, technical and analytical abilities; factual, calm and independent personality with research and practical motivation.

COMPUTER OPERATOR Variable abilities with strong acuity skills and a passive personality with administrative interests.

COMPUTER PROGRAMMER Above average analytical abilities, a factual and independent personality, with research and administrative motivation.

CONFECTIONER Variable abilities with a useful bias towards the perceptual; creative and practical motivation. Personality varies according to the type of employment organisation.

CONFERENCE EXECUTIVE Verbal, numerical and acuity abilities; factual, calm and frequently independent personality, with literary, executive motivation.

COPYWRITER Strong verbal ability with independent personality and literary motivation.

COST ACCOUNTANT Above average numerical ability with factual, calm personality and administrative motivation.

COURIER Variable abilities, aggressive and independent personality, social and administrative motivation.

CURATOR Above average ability; SCPI personality with creative and research motivation.

CUSTOMS OFFICER Above average general abilities (with strong numerical skills if in the VAT section); FCAI personality and practical and administrative motivation.

DANCER Various abilities with an SLAI personality and creative motivation.

DECORATOR Technical and spatial abilities with an FLP personality and practical motivation.

DEMONSTRATOR Technical and spatial abilities with an SLAC personality and executive, practical motivation.

DENTAL ASSISTANT General abilities, often with spatial and acuity strengths; FLPG personality and social and practical motivation.

DENTAL HYGIENIST Above average spatial and technical abilities; factual, lively and often group personality with social and practical motivation.

DENTAL NURSE see NURSE, but with more 'office' hours.

DENTAL TECHNICIAN Technical ability with a factual, calm personality and practical motivation.

DENTIST Well above average spatial and technical abilities; an FCAI personality, with social and research motivation.

DESIGN ENGINEER Numerical and spatial abilities to well above average level, with variable personality depending on employment organisation and a creative and practical motivation.

DESIGNER Above average ability, frequently with spatial skills, an independent, sensitive personality and creative motivation.

DIETICIAN Well above average ability, often with perceptual and analytical strengths: FLPI personality and research motivation.

DIRECTOR (MEDIA) Variable abilities, often sensitive and independent personality and creative and executive motivation.

DISC JOCKEY Variable abilities, with an SLPI personality and social and practical motivation.

DISPENSING OPTICIAN Above average perceptual and spatial abilities, often with acuity skills; a calm and independent personality and executive and research motivation.

DISPLAY ARTIST Spatial ability; often sensitive, lively, independent personality and creative and practical motivation.

DIVER Technical ability, with an FCPI personality and practical motivation.

DOCTOR Well above average numerical, perceptual and analytical abilities; FCAG personality and social motivation.

DRAUGHTSMAN Above average numerical, spatial and acuity abilities with a calm and factual personality and creative and research motivation.

DRESSER (STAGE) Variable abilities; calm, sensitive personality with creative and practical motivation.

DRESSMAKER Spatial ability; SCPI personality and creative motivation.

DRIVER Variable abilities with an FCPI personality and practical motivation.

ECONOMIST Well above average verbal and numerical abilities, research motivation and a variable personality depending on working environment.

EDITOR Verbal and spatial abilities with an independent and aggressive personality and literary and executive motivation.

EDUCATIONAL PSYCHOLOGIST Well above average ability; calm, independent personality and creative and research motivation, together with teaching qualification and experience with disturbed children.

ELECTRICAL ENGINEER Above average spatial and technical abilities and research and practical motivation. Personality more variable, but frequently factual and independent.

ELECTRICIAN Technical ability and variable personality with practical motivation.

EMBALMER Variable abilities; factual, calm, passive personality with creative and practical motivation.

EMPLOYMENT OFFICER Above average general ability, usually with a calm, factual personality and social and administrative motivation.

ENGINEERING PATTERN MAKER Spatial and technical abilities with a creative, practical motivation. Personality more variable, depending on employment environment.

ENGINEERING TECHNICIAN Above average numerical and technical abilities, with factual and independent personality and practical motivation.

ENGRAVER Technical and spatial abilities; passive and independent personality and creative and practical motivation.

ENTERTAINMENTS OFFICER Variable abilities, with a group-orientated and aggressive personality and literary and administrative motivation.

ENVIRONMENTAL HEALTH OFFICER Well above average ability frequently with perceptual and analytical strengths; a factual and independent personality and research and practical motivation.

ERGONOMIST Well above average spatial and analytical abilities, with a calm and often independent personality and research and practical motivation.

ESTATE AGENT Variable abilities, FLAG personality and executive and practical motivation.

ESTATE MANAGER Variable abilities (but increasingly professionally qualified), with a factual, calm and often aggressive personality and executive and administrative motivation.

EXHIBITION ORGANISER *see* CONFERENCE EXECUTIVE.

FARMER Above average ability, particularly in perceptual or technical areas, frequently factual, aggressive and independent personality and practical motivation.

FARM MANAGER As for FARMER, but with additional executive motivation.

FARM SECRETARY Verbal, numerical and acuity abilities with an FCPG personality and practical and administrative motivation.

FARMWORKER Variable abilities, SCPI personality and practical motivation.

FASHION BUYER Variable abilities, usually with spatial skills, with an independent and aggressive (frequently lively) personality and creative and executive motivation.

FASHION DESIGNER Spatial ability; lively, aggressive and independent personality with creative and practical motivation.

FILM PROJECTIONIST Technical ability with an independent and calm personality; creative and practical motivation.

FILM REVIEWER Verbal ability; independent personality and creative and literary motivation.

**187**

FINANCIAL ANALYST Above average numerical and analytical abilities with executive and administrative motivation but more variable personality, depending on working environment.

FINANCIAL CONTROLLER Numerical and acuity ability; factual, calm and aggressive personality and administrative motivation.

FIREMAN Variable abilities; an FCPG personality and practical motivation.

FISHERMAN Variable abilities with a factual and often passive personality and practical motivation.

FITTER Technical ability and practical motivation, with variable but usually factual personality.

FLORIST Spatial ability and sensitive and independent personality with creative motivation.

FLYMAN (THEATRE) Variable abilities; calm and independent personality and creative and practical motivation.

FORENSIC SCIENTIST Well above average perceptual and analytical abilities with a factual, calm and independent personality and research motivation.

FORESTER Technical ability, strong independent personality, frequently calm; factual and practical motivation with a preference for the outdoor life.

FUNERAL DIRECTOR Technical and acuity abilities; calm and independent personality with a balanced factual/sensitive score and social and executive motivation.

FURNITURE MAKER Spatial and technical abilities, often with an independent, calm personality and practical motivation.

GAMEKEEPER Variable abilities and passive and independent personality; practical motivation; prepared to be isolated and out in all weathers.

GARDENER Variable abilities but a technical strength often helps; an SCPI personality with creative and practical motivation.

GENEALOGIST Above average verbal and analytical abilities; factual and independent personality and research and literary motivation.

GENETICIST Well above average perceptual and analytical abilities and research motivation. Personality variable but often factual and independent.

GEOCHEMIST Well above average perceptual and analytical abilities with factual, often independent, personality and research and practical motivation.

GEOLOGIST see GEOCHEMIST.

GEOPHYSICIST see GEOCHEMIST.

GLAZIER Technical ability with an often factual and independent personality and practical motivation.

GOLDSMITH Spatial and technical abilities, often passive and independent personality and creative motivation.

GRAPHIC DESIGNER Spatial and acuity abilities and creative motivation. Personality more variable, but often sensitive and independent.

GROCER Variable abilities; factual, lively and group-orientated personality with practical and administrative motivation.

GROUNDSMAN Variable abilities but often technical strengths; SCPI personality with practical motivation.

GUARD Variable abilities with an FCPG personality and practical abilities.

GUNSMITH Technical ability, often passive and independent personality and practical motivation.

HAIRDRESSER Spatial ability with an FLPG personality and social and practical motivation.

HEAD TEACHER Verbal and numerical abilities (usually above average) and social and executive motivation. Personality tends to be more balanced than clearly defined.

HEALTH VISITOR Above average ability; calm, independent personality and social motivation.

HEATING ENGINEER Perceptual and technical abilities (above average for professional qualification); factual and independent personality and practical motivation.

HISTORIAN Above average acuity and analytical abilities with a passive and factual personality and literary motivation.

HOROLOGIST Technical ability; frequently calm and independent personality with practical motivation.

HOSPITAL PHYSICIST Above average perceptual and technical abilities with a factual, calm and often independent personality and social and practical motivation.

HOSPITAL PORTER Variable abilities; SCPG personality and social and practical motivation.

HOSTEL WARDEN Variable abilities, calm and factual personality with social and often practical motivation.

HOTEL MANAGER Variable abilities, but strengths in verbal and numerical areas helpful; FLAG personality and social and executive motivation.

HOUSE PARENT Variable abilities; FLPG personality, social and practical motivation.

HOUSING MANAGER Above average ability; factual, calm and independent personality (but not passive) and social and administrative motivation.

HUMAN RESOURCES CONSULTANT/DIRECTOR *see* PERSONNEL DIRECTOR.

HYDROGRAPHIC SURVEYOR Above average spatial and technical abilities; factual and independent personality with practical and administrative motivation.

HYDROLOGIST Well above average ability, especially in the perceptual and analytical areas with factual and frequently independent personality and a research and practical motivation.

ILLUSTRATOR Varied abilities, but often spatial skills; sensitive and passive personality with creative motivation.

IMPORT/EXPORT AGENT Variable abilities, but numerical and acuity skills useful; FLALA personality and executive motivation.

INDUSTRIAL DESIGNER Spatial and technical abilities with a varying personality, depending on the particular working environment; creative motivation.

INDUSTRIAL NURSE Above average ability, with a calm and reasonably factual personality and social and practical motivation.

INDUSTRIAL RELATIONS OFFICER Variable abilities, usually factual, independent and calm personality and social and administrative motivation.

INDUSTRIAL SAFETY OFFICER Variable abilities, factual and independent personality (usually more aggressive than passive) with practical and administrative motivation.

INFORMATION SCIENTIST Well above average level of ability (frequently technical and analytical strengths); calm, independent and passive personality and literary and research motivation.

INSTRUMENT AND CONTROL ENGINEER Above average ability, often numerical, technical and analytical skills. Variable personality, depending on the working environment, but usually factual and independent with practical and research motivation.

INSTRUMENT MAKER Numerical and technical abilities, often a factual and independent personality with practical motivation.

INSURANCE AGENT Variable abilities but often numerical and verbal skills; an independent, passive and factual personality with executive and administrative motivation.

INTERIOR DESIGNER Variable abilities (often spatial strengths), an SLAI personality and creative motivation.

INTERPRETER Well above average verbal ability with an FLPI personality and literary motivation.

INTERVIEWER Verbal abilities with a group-orientated and often lively personality and literary and social motivation.

IRONMONGER Variable abilities (numerical and technical are useful); often factual, lively and independent personality and executive and practical motivation.

JEWELLERY MAKER Spatial and acuity abilities with a passive and calm personality; creative, practical motivation.

JOINER Technical ability and practical motivation, but personality would vary according to the kind of working environment.

JOURNALIST Verbal ability with either an SLAG or SCAI personality (depending on the amount of contact with other people expected in the everyday work environment); literary motivation necessary.

JUSTICE'S CLERK Verbal and acuity abilities (usually above average) with a factual, calm and independent personality and administrative motivation.

LABORATORY TECHNICIAN Above average ability (particularly in analytical and perceptual areas) with technical skills for some laboratories. Personality will be variable, but usually factual and passive with strong research motivation.

LANDSCAPE ARCHITECT Above average ability, particularly spatial, with an independent and aggressive personality and practical and creative motivation.

LANGUAGE TEACHER Above average ability; often factual and aggressive personality with literary and social motivation.

LEGAL EXECUTIVE Above average verbal, numerical and acuity abilities. Often factual and slightly aggressive personality with literary and administrative motivation.

LEISURE CENTRE STAFF Variable abilities and usually a lively and independent personality with practical and administrative motivation.

LIBERAL STUDIES TEACHER Above average verbal ability, SLAG personality and social and literary motivation.

LIBRARIAN Well above average verbal ability; SCAI personality and literary motivation.

LIBRARY ASSISTANT Above average verbal ability, an SCPI personality and literary and administrative motivation.

LIGHTHOUSE KEEPER Variable abilities but technical and acuity skills both help. SCPI personality and practical motivation with low social scores. (The job is being phased out by new technology.)

LIGHTING TECHNICIAN (THEATRE) Above average technical ability with a calm and independent personality and creative, practical motivation.

LINGUIST Well above average verbal ability with literary motivation, but personality more variable depending on the working environment.

LITERARY AGENT Verbal ability; calm, independent and practical personality with literary and executive motivation.

LITERARY CRITIC Verbal ability, independent and sensitive personality and literary motivation.

LOCK KEEPER Variable abilities, often factual, calm and independent personality with practical motivation.

LOCKSMITH Spatial and technical abilities with practical motivation and variable (often factual) personality.

LORRY DRIVER *see* TRUCK DRIVER.

MAINTENANCE TECHNICIAN Technical ability with an FLPI personality and practical motivation.

MAKE-UP ARTIST Variable abilities (often spatial) with a sensitive, calm and independent personality and creative motivation.

MANAGEMENT CONSULTANT Above average verbal and analytical abilities with a factual, calm and independent personality and executive motivation.

MANAGEMENT SERVICES ANALYST Above average analytical ability (often verbal and numerical strengths). Factual personality and practical and administrative motivation.

MANAGING DIRECTOR Usually above average abilities with particular strengths and numerical and verbal; SCAI personality with executive motivation.

MARINE BIOLOGIST Well above average perceptual and analytical abilities; often independent personality with research motivation.

MARKET GARDENER Variable abilities, but often spatial and technical strengths, with an independent and passive personality and practical motivation.

MARKETING DIRECTOR/MANAGER Verbal and numerical skills, FLAI personality and executive motivation.

MARKET RESEARCHER Acuity and analytical abilities with a factual, calm and independent personality and research and administrative motivation.

MASSEUR/MASSEUSE FLPG personality and social and practical motivation, but abilities are more variable.

MATERIALS SCIENTIST Above average ability (often perceptual and analytical supported by technical skills); research motivation but personality more variable (although often factual and independent).

MATHEMATICIAN Numerical and analytical skills and well above average ability, often factual and independent personality with research and administrative motivation.

MECHANIC Technical ability, often factual personality and practical motivation.

MECHANICAL ENGINEER Well above average numerical and technical abilities with practical motivation and variable personality, depending on working environment.

MEDICAL ILLUSTRATOR Perceptual and spatial abilities; factual, calm and frequently independent personality with creative and research motivation.

MEDICAL RECORDS OFFICER Perceptual and acuity abilities with social and administrative motivation but variable personality, depending on type of working environment.

MEDICAL REPRESENTATIVE Verbal and perceptual abilities; factual, independent and aggressive personality and executive and research motivation.

MEDICAL SECRETARY Perceptual and acuity abilities, social and administrative motivation but with more variable personality – although often calm and aggressive.

MENTAL NURSE Above average all round ability, SCPG personality and social motivation.

MERCHANDISER Spatial and acuity abilities; often factual, independent and aggressive personality with creative and administrative motivation.

MERCHANT SEAMAN Variable abilities (often technical strengths) with a reasonably factual and group-orientated personality and practical motivation.

METALLURGIST Well above average technical and analytical abilities; factual (often independent) personality, research and practical motivation.

METEOROLOGIST Well above average ability, factual and often independent personality and research motivation.

MICROBIOLOGIST *see* BIOLOGIST.

MIDWIFE Above average ability; calm, independent and moderately aggressive personality with social motivation.

MILKMAN Variable abilities (numerical skills help), SCPI personality and practical and social motivation.

MILLER Variable abilities, but technical and acuity skills help. Often factual and independent personality with practical and research motivation.

MILLINER Spatial ability with variable personality and practical motivation.

MINER Variable abilities, calm and group-orientated personality, practical motivation.

MINISTER OF RELIGION Verbal ability; factual, calm and independent personality and social and administrative motivation.

MODEL (FASHION/GRAPHIC) Variable abilities with SLPI personality.

MODEL MAKER Technical ability supported by spatial skills; SLAI personality with practical motivation.

MUSEUM ASSISTANT Variable abilities (often spatial and technical skills help at professional level) with a calm and passive personality and creative and research motivation.

MUSICIAN (ORCHESTRAL) Above average ability with an SLAI personality and creative motivation. Talent also helps!

MUSIC THERAPIST Above average ability with a sensitive and lively personality and social and creative motivation.

NANNY Variable abilities; SCPI personality and social motivation.

NATURE CONSERVANCY WARDEN Variable abilities, with spatial and technical helpful; independent personality and practical motivation.

NAVIGATING OFFICER Spatial and acuity abilities, with factual, calm and independent personality and research and practical motivation.

NEGOTIATOR Variable abilities (numerical skills help); often aggressive and independent personality and executive motivation.

NOVELIST Verbal ability, strongly independent personality and literary motivation plus talent and luck!

NUCLEAR PHYSICIST Above average numerical and perceptual abilities, often factual, calm and independent personality; research and practical motivation.

NURSE Above average ability with an FCPG personality and social and research motivation.

NURSERY NURSE SCPG personality and social motivation.

NUTRITIONIST Above average perceptual and analytical abilities; factual and lively personality and research and social motivation.

OCCUPATIONAL PSYCHOLOGIST Well above average verbal and analytical abilities, usually factual lively and independent personality with social and research motivation.

OCCUPATIONAL THERAPIST Above average abilities (particularly technical and acuity skills); calm and independent personality with social and practical motivation.

OFFICE CLEANER Variable abilities, with an often independent and lively personality and practical motivation.

OFFICE MACHINERY MECHANIC Technical ability with an FLPI personality and practical and administrative motivation.

OFFICE MANAGER Numerical and acuity abilities; factual but not passive personality and administrative and executive motivation.

OIL RIG WORKER Technical ability; factual and independent personality and practical motivation.

OPERATIONAL RESEARCHER Well above average numerical ability with an FCPI personality and research and administrative motivation.

OPHTHALMIC OPTICIAN Above average ability (particularly in spatial and acuity areas); often factual and independent personality with research and social motivation.

OPTICIAN *see* DISPENSING OPTICIAN.

ORGANISATION AND METHODS OFFICER *see* WORK STUDY OFFICER.

ORTHOPTIST Above average technical ability with a calm (but not sensitive) personality social and research motivation.

OSTEOPATH Above average ability, an SCAG personality and social motivation.

PANEL BEATER Spatial and technical abilities, a variable personality, depending on working environment, and practical motivation.

PATENT AGENT Verbal and technical abilities (usually above average); with an FCPI personality and practical and literary motivation.

PATENT EXAMINER Above average technical and analytical abilities; factual, calm and independent personality with practical and research motivation.

PATHOLOGIST Well above average perceptual and analytic abilities (supported by acuity skills); factual, independent personality (often calm and aggressive) with research and practical motivation.

PATTERN CUTTER Spatial and technical abilities, often factual and passive personality with practical motivation.

PERSONNEL DIRECTOR Verbal ability and an SCAI personality with executive motivation.

PERSONNEL OFFICER Verbal and acuity abilities and social motivation. Personality is more variable, but often factual and lively.

PHARMACIST Well above average perceptual and acuity abilities; factual, independent (often aggressive) personality and research and social motivation.

PHARMACOLOGIST Well above average perceptual and acuity abilities with a factual and independent personality and research motivation.

PHILOSOPHER Well above average verbal and analytical abilities and literary motivation. Personality more variable, but usually independent.

PHOTOGRAPHER Spatial abilities with an independent personality and creative and research motivation.

PHOTOGRAPHIC TECHNICIAN Technical and acuity abilities, often with a calm and independent personality and practical motivation.

PHYSICAL EDUCATION TEACHER Above average ability; usually factual, lively personality and social and practical motivation.

PHYSICIST Well above average numerical and technical abilities, factual personality (frequently independent), research and practical motivation.

PHYSIOTHERAPIST Above average ability with a calm, independent personality and social and practical motivation.

PIANO TUNER Acuity ability; often sensitive and calm personality with practical motivation.

PICTURE FRAMER Spatial ability; often independent and passive personality and creative and practical motivation.

PLASTERER Spatial ability with variable personality (often calm and independent) with practical motivation.

PLAY LEADER Variable abilities with an FLPG personality and social motivation.

PLUMBER Spatial and technical abilities; variable personality (often factual and independent) with practical motivation.

POET Verbal ability with a sensitive and independent personality and literary motivation.

POLICE OFFICER Above average ability with an FCPG personality and social and practical motivation.

POLITICAL AGENT Variable abilities with an FLAG personality and executive motivation.

POLITICIAN Verbal ability, FLAG personality and executive motivation.

POSTER DESIGNER *see* GRAPHIC DESIGNER.

POSTMAN/WOMAN Variable abilities with a calm and independent personality, social and practical motivation.

POST OFFICE CLERK Numerical ability, often factual, passive and group-orientated personality with administrative motivation.

POTTER Spatial ability with an SCPI personality and creative and practical motivation.

PRESS AGENT *see* LITERARY AGENT.

PRIEST/CLERGYMAN *see* MINISTER OF RELIGION.

PRINCIPAL NURSING OFFICER Above average ability; SCAG personality, social and administraive motivation.

PRINTER Spatial and technical abilities with independent personality and a literary and practical motivation.

PRISON OFFICER Variable abilities with an FCPG personality and social and practical motivation.

PROBATION OFFICER Variable abilities with a factual personality and social motivation.

PRODUCER (FILMS ETC) Variable ability (numerical skills helpful); factual and independent personality (often aggressive), literary and executive motivation.

PRODUCTION MANAGER Above average technical and numerical abilities with an FCAG personality and executive and practical motivation.

PROGRAMMER *see* COMPUTER PROGRAMMER.

PROOF READER Above average verbal and acuity abilities with a passive and independent personality and literary motivation.

PROPERTY NEGOTIATOR Numerical and verbal abilities with an FLAI personality and executive motivation.

PSYCHIATRIC SOCIAL WORKER Variable abilities; factual, aggressive and group-orientated personality and social motivation.

PSYCHO-ANALYST Above average verbal ability with an SCPI personality and social motivation.

PSYCHOLOGIST Above average verbal and analytical abilities with an SLAI or SCAG personality and social motivation.

PSYCHO-THERAPIST Variable abilities (above average for professional qualifications); SCPG personality with literary and social motivation.

PUBLICAN Variable abilities (numerical skills help); FCAG personality and executive and practical motivation.

PUBLICITY AGENT Verbal and numerical abilities with an aggressive and group-orientated personality and executive motivation.

PUBLIC RELATIONS EXECUTIVE Verbal ability with FLAG personality and literary and executive motivation.

PUBLIC RELATIONS DIRECTOR/MANAGER Above average verbal ability with an SLAG personality and executive motivation.

PUBLISHER Verbal and spatial abilities with an FLAI personality and literary and executive motivation.

PURSER Above average numerical ability; independent and aggressive personality and administrative motivation. (This position increasingly requires professional accountancy qualifications.)

QUALITY CONTROLLERS Above average technical and analytical abilities with factual and independent personality and research and practical motivation.

QUALITY INSPECTORS Technical and acuity abilities, often independent personality and practical motivation.

QUANTITY SURVEYOR Well above average numerical and technical abilities with a factual, passive and independent personality and practical and administrative motivation.

RADIOGRAPHER Above average ability with perceptual and spatial skills particularly useful; normally a calm and independent personality with scientific and research motivation.

RADIO PRESENTER *see* TELEVISION AND RADIO PRESENTER.

RAILWAY GUARD Mixed abilities with a factual, calm and often independent personality and social and practical motivation.

RATING VALUATION OFFICER Above average ability (numerical specialisation helpful); FCPI personality and practical and administrative motivation.

RECEPTIONIST Variable abilities (acuity, numerical and verbal strengths useful); variable personality according to employment environment (often calm and slightly aggressive), literary and administrative motivation.

REMEDIAL TEACHER Above average ability with an SCPG personality and social motivation.

REPORTER Above average ability, particularly verbal, with aggressive, independent personality and literary motivation.

RESTORER Variable abilities (spatial and technical skills help), often with a calm and independent personality and creative and research motivation.

RETAIL MANAGER Variable abilities (numerical skills useful); FCAG personality and social and executive motivation.

ROOFER Spatial and technical abilities, often with a calm, aggressive and independent personality and practical motivation.

SADDLER Spatial ability with a variable personality, depending on occupational environment, but often independent with practical motivation.

SAILOR (MERCHANT NAVY) *see* MERCHANT SEAMAN.

SALES EXECUTIVE Verbal ability with a lively but not passive personality and executive and administrative motivation.

SALES MANAGER Verbal (and often numerical) abilities with an FLAG personality and executive motivation.

SALESPERSON Verbal ability with group-orientated personality and social and executive motivation.

SALES TRAINER Variable abilities (often verbal strengths) with a factual and often aggressive personality and social motivation.

SCIENCE TEACHER Above average ability (particularly in perceptual and verbal areas) with a calm and factual personality and social and research motivation.

SCIENCE WRITER Verbal and perceptual abilities with a factual and independent personality and literary and research motivation.

SCIENTIFIC INSTRUMENT MAKER Perceptual and technical abilities with an FCPI personality and research and practical motivation.

SCULPTOR Spatial ability, and SLAI personality. Creative and practical motivation, and talent!

SECRETARY/PA Verbal and acuity abilities with literary and administrative motivation. Personality is more variable, depending on work environment, but will often be calm and moderately independent.

SECURITIES ANALYST Above average analytical and numerical abilities with a factual and independent personality and administrative motivation.

SECURITY OFFICER Variable abilities with a factual, calm and independent personality. Practical and administrative motivation.

SESSION MUSICIAN Variable abilities with an SCAI personality and creative motivation; plus talent and luck!

SET DESIGNER Spatial and technical abilities, often with a sensitive and independent personality and creative motivation.

SEWING MACHINIST Variable abilities; often passive and group-orientated personality and practical motivation.

SHEPHERD Variable abilities; SCPI personality and practical motivation together with a love of the outdoor life.

SHIPPING AND FORWARDING OFFICER Verbal and numerical abilities with administrative motivation. Personality more variable, depending on occupational environment.

SHIPPING PILOT Numerical and spatial abilities often with excellent acuity skills. Often calm and independent personality and practical motivation.

SHOP ASSISTANT Variable abilities (numerical and acuity skills useful); SLPI personality and executive motivation.

SHOP FITTER Spatial and acuity abilities; variable personality, but often sensitive and independent with creative and practical motivation.

SIGN WRITER Verbal, spatial and acuity abilities; often a sensitive, calm and independent personality with creative and practical motivation.

SILVERSMITH Spatial and technical abilities; sensitive, passive and independent personality with creative and some practical motivation.

SLATER *see* ROOFER.

SOCIAL SCIENTIST Above average ability with an SCAI personality and social and research motivation.

SOCIAL WORKER Above average abilities with an SCAG personality and social and administrative motivation.

SOLDIER Variable abilities (increasingly technical skills required) with an FCPG personality and social and practical motivation.

SOLICITOR Well above average verbal ability, FCAI personality and literary and administrative motivation.

SOUND ENGINEER Above average technical and numerical abilities with variable personality, but often aggressive and independent. Creative and practical motivation.

SPEECH AND DRAMA TEACHER Above average verbal abilities. Sensitive and aggressive personality and social and literary motivation.

SPEECH THERAPIST Well above average ability. Sensitive, independent and often lively personality with literary and social motivation.

SPORTS COACH Variable abilities and often a lively, aggressive personality with social and practical motivation.

STAGE DESIGNER *see* SET DESIGNER.

STAGE-HAND Variable abilities; calm personality (often slightly aggressive and group biased) with creative and practical motivation.

STAGE MANAGER Variable abilities (increasingly technical strengths); calm, aggressive and independent personality with a literary and practical motivation.

STATISTICIAN Well above average numerical abilities (acuity skills needed for a statistics producer and analytical for an analyst). Factual and independent personality with research and administrative motivation.

STOCK CONTROLLER Numerical and acuity abilities with a variable personality, depending upon employment environment, but often factual, passive and independent, with practical and administrative motivation.

STONE-MASON Spatial abilities with an often independent, sensitive personality and creative motivation.

STOREKEEPER *see* STOCK CONTROLLER.

STUDIO ASSISTANT Variable abilities (often technical skills needed); passive and independent personality (often lively) with creative and social motivation.

SURGEON Well above average ability (particularly in perceptual and analytical areas); calm, independent personality with research motivation.

SURVEYOR Numerical and spatial abilities with factual and calm personality (often independent) and research and practical motivation.

SYSTEMS ANALYST Well above average numerical and analytical abilities; FCPI personality and research and administrative motivation.

TAILOR Spatial abilities with a variable personality, depending on occupational environment, and practical motivation.

TAXIDERMIST Variable abilities (often spatial and technical strengths); calm and independent personality with practical motivation.

TAXI-DRIVER Variable abilities; a lively and often aggressive personality (but not strongly group-orientated) with social and practical motivation.

TAX INSPECTOR Above average numerical abilities; factual, independent (often aggressive) personality with executive and administrative motivation.

TEACHER Above average ability (often verbal strengths) with an SCAG personality and social motivation.

TEACHER OF FINE ART AND CRAFTS Similar to teacher, but with higher spatial ability and social and creative motivation.

TEACHER OF HANDICAPPED Similar to teacher, but with less emphasis on verbal skills.

TECHNICAL REPRESENTATIVE Verbal and technical abilities with factual, independent and sometimes aggressive personality and executive and research motivation.

TECHNICAL WRITER Above average verbal and technical abilities. Independent, calm and often passive personality and literary and practical or research motivation.

TELECOMMUNICATIONS ENGINEER Numerical and technical abilities. Factual personality, often lively and group-orientated with practical motivation.

TELEPHONIST Variable abilities but acuity skills useful; lively, group-orientated personality most predominant with social and practical motivation.

TELEVISION ENGINEER Numerical and technical abilities (usually above average) with a factual and independent often aggressive personality and practical motivation.

TELEVISION PRODUCTION ASSISTANT Variable ability but acuity skills useful, with a calm and independent personality and creative and literary motivation.

TELEVISION OR RADIO PRESENTER Verbal ability with a lively, independent personality and creative and executive motivation.

THATCHER Spatial ability with an SCPI personality and practical motivation.

THEATRE ADMINISTRATOR Above average verbal and numerical abilities; calm and independent personality with creative and administrative motivation.

TILER Spatial and acuity abilities with a calm (often independent) personality and practical motivation.

TOOL MAKER Technical and numerical abilities, factual and independent personality and practical motivation.

TOY MAKER Technical and spatial abilities with practical motivation. Personality more variable according to employment environment.

TRACER Spatial and acuity abilities; FLAI personality and practical and administrative motivation.

TRADER Variable abilities (numerical skills useful) with a factual and lively personality and practical motivation.

TRAFFIC WARDEN Variable abilities; factual and independent personality. Practical and administrative motivation.

TRAIN DRIVER Variable abilities; calm and independent personality and practical motivation.

TRAINING OFFICER Above average general ability; SCAI personality and social and practical motivation.

TRANSLATOR Verbal and acuity abilities; variable personality (but often sensitive, calm and independent), literary and administrative motivation.

TRANSPORT MANAGER Variable abilities, an FCAG personality and executive and practical motivation.

TRAVEL AGENT Verbal and numerical abilities with often a factual, lively and moderately independent personality and executive and administrative motivation.

TRUCK DRIVER Variable abilities with an FCPI personality and practical motivation.

TURF ACCOUNTANT Above average numerical ability with an FLPI personality and executive and administrative motivation.

TYPIST Acuity skills are predominant but verbal ability is useful; variable personality depending on employment environment, and administrative motivation.

UNDERTAKER see FUNERAL DIRECTOR.

UNDERWRITER Above average numerical abilities. Independent and factual personality. Administrative and executive motivation.

UNION NEGOTIATOR Variable abilities with an SLAG personality and executive motivation.

UPHOLSTERER Spatial ability with an often calm and independent personality and practical motivation.

VETERINARY NURSE Variable abilities. Sensitive and usually calm and independent personality and practical motivation.

VETERINARY SURGEON Well above average ability; independent and moderately sensitive personality with executive and research motivation.

VISION MIXER Above average spatial and technical abilities; calm personality and creative motivation.

WAITER/WAITRESS Variable abilities; SLPI personality and social and practical motivation.

WATCH AND CLOCK REPAIRER Spatial and technical abilities; often calm and independent personality and practical motivation.

WINDOW DRESSER Spatial ability, sensitive (often lively and independent) personality and creative motivation.

WORD PROCESSOR OPERATOR Verbal and acuity abilities, variable personality according to employment environment but often factual and passive, with administrative motivation.

WORK STUDY OFFICER Above average ability with an FCAI personality and research and practical motivation.

WRITER Verbal ability, independent personality and literary motivation.

YOUTH WORKER Variable ability, SCAG personality and social (often practical) motivation.

ZOO KEEPER Variable ability with calm and independent personality and practical motivation.

ZOOLOGIST Well above average perceptual (and often numerical) abilities, usually with a calm, independent and passive personality and research motivation.

1876